THE RISE OF URBAN AMERICA

ADVISORY EDITOR
Richard C. Wade

PROFESSOR OF AMERICAN HISTORY
UNIVERSITY OF CHICAGO

MODERN CITIES
AND THEIR
RELIGIOUS PROBLEMS

Samuel Lane Loomis

ARNO PRESS

&

The New York Times

NEW YORK · 1970

Reprint Edition 1970 by Arno Press Inc.

Reprinted from a copy in The University of Illinois Library

LC# 73-112558
ISBN 0-405-02464-9

THE RISE OF URBAN AMERICA
ISBN for complete set 0-405-02430-4

Manufactured in the United States of America

MODERN CITIES

AND

Their Religious Problems

BY

SAMUEL LANE LOOMIS.

WITH AN INTRODUCTION

BY

REV. JOSIAH STRONG, D.D.

NEW YORK:

THE BAKER & TAYLOR COMPANY,

740 AND 742 BROADWAY.

Printed by Edward O. Jenkins' Sons,
20 North William St., New York.

PREFATORY NOTE.

THE following chapters, with the exception of the sixth, comprise a course of lectures which were prepared for the students of Andover Theological Seminary, and delivered at Andover in November, 1886. The third chapter had also previously been used as a lecture, in Cincinnati, before the students of Lane Theological Seminary. The greater part of the first, second, fourth, and fifth chapters subsequently appeared in the *Andover Review*, with whose kind permission they are reprinted here. The whole matter, with considerable additions and some changes, is now respectfully offered to the public in the hope that it may contribute to the general information and deepen the general interest in the great subject with which it deals, and may thus help to prepare the way for the adoption of more earnest and systematic efforts looking toward the advancement of the Redeemer's kingdom among the neglected masses of the great towns.

BROOKLYN, N. Y., *July* 1, 1887.

INTRODUCTION.

THE city is the Gibraltar of civilization. It is not because our urban population is nearly or quite one-fourth of the whole that it is being made the object of special study. The writer of this book sees that the city is strategic; and in directing our attention and effort to the strategic point, we are following a divine example. When God looked down upon this earth to select a native land for Christianity, he laid his finger on that country in which the highways of the nations met. The world's altar was erected at that point—the point where the three great civilizations which were to exert the profoundest influence upon the world, the Jewish, the Greek, and the Roman, came into the completest conjunction. That fact was illustrated by the inscription over the Cross, written in Greek, in Hebrew, and in Latin, that all the motley crowd might read. The place where the Cross of Christ was planted was a strategic point. The Lord Jesus Christ set us this example when he bade his disciples begin at the metropolis. That word was remembered by the Apostles when they went forth to plant churches in Antioch, in Ephesus, in Athens, in Corinth, and in Rome.

The city is the great centre of influence in modern civilization, as it has been in all civilizations. In the city is massed the mighty power of wealth, with its far-reaching influence. In the city are located the great corporations with their marvelous power over the whole land. In the city live the owners of most of the mining and railway stocks, and from the city these mines and railways, with their armies of employés, are controlled. In the city is the press—that tree of the knowledge of good and evil, whose leaves are not altogether for the " *healing* of the nations." The city, then, is the great center of influence, both good and bad. It contains that which is fairest and foulest in our civilization. It is the mighty heart of the body politic, which sends its streams of life pulsating to the very finger-tips of the whole land ; and when the blood becomes poisoned, it poisons every fiber of the whole body. Hence the supreme importance of city evangelization.

But there is special need of evangelizing the city because the city is exposed to special perils. There are great perils threatening our Christian civilization, such as wealth, its worship and its congestion, anarchism and lawlessness, intemperance and the liquor power, immigration and a superstitious Christianity; all these threaten the land as a whole, and these are all massed in the cities. And not only so, but in the city every one of these perils is enhanced. Take as an illustration, immigration, which is intimately connected with most of the other perils. Our ten larger cities contain only nine per cent. of the entire population, but nearly one-quarter of the foreign. A little less than one-third of the population of the United States is foreign by birth or parentage, but this element rarely constitutes less than two-thirds of our larger cities and often more than three-fourths. That is, whatever strain immigration puts upon our institutions is more than twice as great in the cities as in the country. The fact that foreigners are thus massed seems to some an occasion for congratulation. It certainly affords a great opportunity and lays on us a great obligation, but it increases the peril. When foreigners are scattered among the native population, each being surrounded by Americans, they are forced to learn our language and are soon led to adopt our ideas and habits—in short, are speedily Americanized. But when massed in cities, they gather in quarters occupied often exclusively by their own nationality. Our language is not a necessity; they come but little in contact with our life, and old habits and ideas give way but slowly before American influence. If a thousand anarchists were scattered throughout a State, they would be harmless; but when these firebrands of society are brought together in the city, they inflame each other. Whether the massing of the enemy is an advantage or disadvantage to us, depends on the relative strength of the two armies. "Stonewall" Jackson, at the head of 13,000 troops, defeated four armies with an aggregate force of 64,0 0 men in about a month. His generalship showed itself in striking his enemy when separated. "Divide and conquer." Had the Union armies in the Shenandoah Valley been massed, Jackson would have been helpless save to retreat. If our forces are tenfold those of the enemy we may congratulate ourselves that by massing his men he has made their capture easy. But what if his forces are tenfold greater than ours? In six Assembly Districts of New York the aggregate population is 360,000, for which there are thirty-one Protestant churches and 3,018 saloons. For the whole country east of the Mississippi there are nearly as many churches as saloons, but for this population—larger than Cincinnati—there are nearly one hundred times as many saloons as churches. In the First Assembly District of New York there were, in 1880, 44,000 people, seven Protestant churches, and 1,072 saloons—one hundred and fifty-three saloons for every church. These churches are open, probably, seven or eight hours a week, the saloons sixteen or more hours a day. While the Gospel of our Lord Jesus Christ is preached from one church seven or eight hours, the gospel of death and hell is preached from each of a hundred or a hundred and fifty of these "synagogues of Satan" a hundred hours! And the saloon is only one of many arms of the devil's service. We do not give the Gospel the half of a fair chance. What a forlorn hope is a struggle against such odds. To congratulate ourselves before an enemy thus massed is to rejoice in our own defeat, unless we are prepared to order up adequate reinforcements.

It might be shown that each of the perils mentioned above, is much greater in the city than in the country, but it is sufficiently manifest that the city is peculiarly endangered. It is here that we should bring to bear most powerfully the conservative influences of society. The good general strengthens his line opposite those points where the enemy's lines are the strongest. But how is it in the city? Do we find, as a matter of fact, that the two great conserving influences of society—namely, the home and the church—are correspondingly powerful in the city? as much stronger there than in the country, as these perils are there greater than elsewhere? In the country, the great majority live in homes of their own; in the city, the small minority.

In 1880 there were two hundred and forty-three thousand families in New York City, and it was estimated that only thirteen thousand of them lived in their own homes—a fact, which in its bearing on the morals of the city, contains a whole volume of meaning. And as land appreciates in value with the growth of our cities, the relative number of renters will increase. Thus in the city the institution of the home is weak and growing weaker.

As for the church, there are from three to six times as many churches for a given population in the country as in the city; and in our great cities there are large populations nearly or quite destitute. For the twentieth Assembly District in New York, with a population of over sixty thousand, there are but three Protestant churches. In the whole country, for every sixty thousand people there are one hundred and twenty evangelical churches. For one district in New York of fifty thousand souls there is but one Protestant church; and it is said that in the heart of Chicago there are sixty thousand people without a single church, either Protestant or Catholic.

In reply to the assertion that the city is not so well supplied with churches as the country, it is said, and truly, that the city churches are much stronger than those in the country. But it is also true, and decisive of the point in question, that the proportion of evangelical church members is only from one-half to one-fifth as large in the great cities as in the country. And with rare exceptions, if any, church provision seems to

be steadily falling behind the growth of urban population, as indicated by the following table.

	NEWARK, N. J.	JERSEY CITY, N. J.	BROOKLYN.	NEW YORK.
In 1840	1 Prot. Ch. to 955 souls.		1 to 1,575 souls	1 to 2,066 souls
In 1850	1 Prot. Ch. to 1,215 souls.	1 to 827 souls.	1 to 1,760 "	1 to 2,446 "
In 1860	1 Prot. Ch. to 1,263 souls	1 to 935 souls.	1 to 2,035 "	1 to 2,775 "
In 1870	1 Prot. Ch. to 1,590 souls.		1 to 2,085 "	1 to 2,479 "
In 1880	1 Prot. Ch. to 1,684 souls.	1 to 1,873 souls	1 to 2,673 "	1 to 3,046 "
In 1887	1 Prot. Ch. to 1,717 souls.			1 to 3,750* "

If the growth of our great cities were suddenly
arrested, there would still be a grave responsibility rest-
ing on the churches to evangelize neglected districts;
and on the other hand, if our cities had no slums, no
churchless multitudes, their rapid growth would demand a greater Christian activity than now exists, simply to provide for the new-comers. There is a city of
thirty-five thousand added to Chicago, and one of fifty
thousand added to New York every year, for which
there must be Christian provision. In 1880, as we have
seen, there was in New York one Protestant church to
every three thousand people (one-sixth of the average
for the whole country). Simply to have held our own,
without taking one step forward, there should have
been added during these six years one hundred Protestant churches to the Christian forces of the city.

---

* Present population estimated at 1,500,000. But the city directory
just issued makes the population 1,600,000, which gives 4,000 souls
to every Protestant church.

Not one-half or quarter or tenth of that number have been organized. To meet the needs of these three hundred thousand souls only *four* churches have been added. Doubtless there are cities better off than New York and there are others which are worse. It is true of all the cities whose religious statistics the writer has looked up, that their church provision is falling behind the growth of their population.

It is evident that the evangelization of our cities is exceptionally important ; that the cities are exceptionally exposed to perils ; that in them the great conservative influences are exceptionally weak. This volume shows, by its analysis of the social composition of American cities, that in their evangelization we have exceptional difficulties to overcome. What then ? Do such facts justify discouragement ? A discouraged Christian is a spectacle for angels Every believer has a right to take Paul's sublime declaration of confidence as a formula in which to write his own name, " I, ——— ———, can do all things " required of me, " through Jesus Christ, which strengtheneth me." To a mighty faith the heaping up of obstacles is only a stimulus ; the higher they rise, the greater the inspiration.

This volume not only points out the necessity and magnitude and difficulty of the work to be done in our cities, but abounds in valuable suggestions touching methods of work. Because English civilization is older than ours the problem of the city arrested attention and attracted study sooner there than here. In the work of city evangelization we have much to learn from the Christian workers of London and the McAll mission in Paris. This book enables us to profit by their experience and success. Its author, after five years' experience in city work, which made him a good student of its problems, spent the greater part of a year in the heart of London, making himself thoroughly familiar with English methods of city evangelization His presentation of facts is worthy of all the confidence to which careful observation and accuracy of statement are entitled.

It may be objected that English character and conditions so differ from ours that we should not find their methods applicable here. In answer be it said, that Rev. Dr. Rainsford's remarkable work in St. George's Church, New York, affords a practical demonstration to the contrary. His experience shows that English methods are quite adapted, or at least adaptable, to American cities ; and the sooner our churches accept the conclusions of this book, and act on its valuable recommendations, the sooner will the "threat of the cities" cease.

Josiah Strong.

CONTENTS.

CHAPTER III.

THE THREAT OF THE CITIES.

CHAPTER IV.

CHRISTIAN WORK IN LONDON—THE CHURCH OF ENGLAND.

CHAPTER V.

CHRISTIAN WORK IN LONDON—DISSENTING CHURCHES—OTHER MOVEMENTS.

CHAPTER VI.

THE McALL MISSION.

CHAPTER VII.

SUGGESTIONS REGARDING CHRISTIAN WORK FOR OUR CITIES.

CHAPTER I.

WHEN men affirm that history repeats itself, they utter only half a truth. The people of all times are so much alike, and similar situations recur so frequently, that nearly every present event may have some sort of parallel in the past; and yet the current of history is no tide sweeping perpetually up and down the same old channel, but, like some majestic river, it rolls forever onward. No age is a mere repetition of what has gone before it; the main features of each are new, unforeseen, and unparalleled. Greece was not another Egypt, nor Rome another Greece. The decay of the dominion of the Cæsars, the rise of Papacy, the conquests of the False Prophet, the Crusades, the founding of the Frankish empire, the Reformation and Renaissance, the overthrow of feudalism and growth of constitutional liberty,—each of these great movements, with the events that cluster about it, has furnished in its turn a fresh chapter in the world's history quite unmatched by any which had preceded it.

So also is it with our own time. The world in which we live is not merely different from that our fathers knew. It is a world the like of which has never been known by any race of men in any age before. Upon the nineteenth century have fallen certain changes in the social and industrial conditions of mankind of so

2 (17)

great moment, that in consequence of them Christendom has been transformed and the whole aspect of its society changed with almost the swiftness of a revolution. Accompanied by neither clash of arms nor thunder of cannon, the forces which have thus revolutionized society have wrought so silently, that until the last few years they had almost escaped observation. Yet none the less steadily, speedily, and mightily have they done their work, bringing with them results that have filled life with new problems and perils together with fresh opportunities and hopes. These changes are most conspicuously illustrated by the subject with which we deal in this chapter.

We live in the age of great cities. It began to be so named nearly half a century ago,* and every year since then has added fitness to the title. For size, for number, and for influence, the cities of our time have never been approached. Rome has always stood as supreme example of the vast and mighty city. In Gibbon's day, the most populous of modern capitals had not equalled her. But the present Paris is probably much larger than she; the present London more than twice as large, and our own metropolis fully her equal.† And Rome stood alone in her greatness ; she did not, like New York, have a Brooklyn close beside her, a Philadelphia two hours away, and sixty other towns of considerable size within a day's journey. The other large and flour-

---

* *The Age of Great Cities.* Robert Vaughan, London, 1843.

† See Gibbon, vol. iv., chap. 31; also notes in Smith's edition, p. 89, London, 1854. Gibbon estimates the population at 1,200,000; Dureau de la Malle, 562,000; Zumpt, 2,000,000; Hoeck, 2,265,000; *Encyclopædia Britannica,* about 1,000,000.

ishing cities in the empire were few and widely separated.

One of the chief reasons that used formerly to occasion the building of cities has disappeared ; roving bands of robbers and savage beasts are no longer at large ; throughout the civilized world life is as safe in the country as in the town. Security has ceased to be reckoned among the advantages of a city residence.

Much of the loneliness and isolation that once belonged to the country home have also been removed. The extension of railway and telegraph lines, the widening circulation of papers and periodicals, the increased facilities of trade, and many other things, have combined to lessen the inconveniences of rural life, and make it brighter and more attractive.

Moreover, as men have grown in wisdom, their appreciation of natural beauty and the attractions of mountain, field, and forest, have become keener. Nevertheless, each successive year finds a stronger and more irresistible current sweeping in toward the centres of life ; a larger and larger proportion of the earth's inhabitants crowded together in the great cities, and a rural population always diminishing in relative size and influence.

The extent of this movement, and the suddenness with which it has sprung upon the nineteenth century, cannot be better illustrated than by a glance at the growth of the world's metropolis.

London is an ancient as well as a modern town ; it seems to have had at least two thousand years of growth. In Tacitus' day it was already a thriving place, full of merchants and their wares.*

---

* Tac. *Annal.*, lib. 14, chap. 33.

A writer of the third century calls it "illustrious for the vast number of merchants who resorted to it ; for its extensive commerce and for the abundance of every kind of commodity which it could supply." The Venerable Bede, in the eighth century, terms it, " An emporium of many nations who arrived thither by land and sea." By a writer of the sixteenth century, it was said to be " the largest in extent, the fairest built, the most populous, and the best inhabited of any city in the world."

As the greatest of marts, and as capital and metropolis of one of the most remarkable of nations, it has, for a thousand years, held a high place among the chief cities of Christendom. So far as one can judge by old maps and pictures, and such obscure hints as the ancient annals give us, the growth of London, from Roman times until the close of the last century, although very irregular, was most of the time exceedingly slow.*

The London of three hundred years ago seems to have been considerably smaller than the present Boston ; that of two hundred years ago, according to a somewhat careful computation, had reached 670,000 inhabitants,† which is less than the population claimed for Chicago. It took the great city another century to climb to a place equal to that of Philadelphia, and half a century more, bringing it down to 1836, did not make

---

* The old historians give widely varying estimates, which are apparently little more than guesses. An estimate based on the bills of mortality, which first began to be kept at that time, would show a population of something more than 250,000 in the last decade of the 16th century. See discussion of the subject in Stow's *London*, also *Encyclopædia Britannica*, 9th ed., vol. 14, page 820.

† Sir William Petty, *Essay on Political Arithmetic.*

it equal to the present New York, if you include with New York, Brooklyn and Jersey City. But in order to make a city equal in size to the London of to-day, you must pile together New York, Philadelphia, Brooklyn, Chicago, Boston, St. Louis, Baltimore, Cincinnati, and San Francisco.

There are in London—assuming the average annual rate of increase which prevailed between 1860 and 1880 to have continued since the last census—not less than 5,500,000 souls. By London, we mean, in every case, what is called "Greater London," which consists of the metropolitan and city police districts, and extends twelve miles in all directions from Charing Cross.*

In the last hundred and twenty years preceding the year 1800, London increased in size only fifty per cent. In the eighty-six years since the year 1800 London has increased five hundred per cent. More people live in London alone than in the whole of Holland; more than in Sweden; more than in Portugal; more than in Ireland or Canada; more by a million than in Scotland. She could furnish population for two countries like Denmark, and nearly enough for three like Norway. Three cities as large as the greater London would be almost enough to people Spain, with its present population; six would be more than enough to people Italy; seven, nearly enough to people France; and eleven, to people the United States.

It is said that Macaulay, in his time, walked through every street of the metropolis. In order to accomplish

---

* The exact figures of the census of 1881 are 4,766,661, and the average annual rate of increase between '61 and '81 is 2.39 per cent. Inner, or registration London, contained fewer people by 850,000. See *Census of England and Wales* for 1881, vol. iv., p. 13, London, 1883.

that feat now, one would need to take a tramp of
twenty-five hundred miles. Three hundred and fifty
more persons may be expected to sleep in London to-
night than slept there last night; twenty-five hundred
more than a week ago to night. Every month adds a
city of ten thousand inhabitants; every year one of one
hundred and twenty-five thousand inhabitants.

One may be helped to realize the extraordinary expansion which the nineteenth century has witnessed in
the city of the Thames, by considering what would be
the consequence if the same rate of increase should
continue a hundred years longer. Supposing London
to keep on growing for the next century as fast as she
has grown since 1860, by 1985 a population of over
forty millions would be gathered about Charing Cross;
which is more than all Great Britain and Ireland contain. Such a supposition is, of course, introduced only
as an illustration. It does not seem probable that the
great city can continue growing at the present rate
much longer.* Yet we must remember that a London
of forty million people cannot seem more unlikely to
us than one of five millions to the men of a few centuries ago The England of Charles I. had fewer
inhabitants than the London of Victoria. Not until the
days of the Iron Duke had the United Kingdoms gotten
to have a population twice as great as that of the present metropolis.

---

* Although the rate of increase during the last decade was somewhat more rapid than during the period between 1860 and 1870, it is
believed that since 1880 the rate has declined and that it is likely to
continue slowly declining for the next fifty years. See paper on
Population of London, by R. Price Williams, read before Statistical
Society, June 16, 1885, printed with discussion in the journal of that
society, London, 1885.

But London is by no means the only English city. Huge as she is, she contains only one-third of the city population of the island. There are in England and Wales alone, twenty-seven other great cities, the smallest of which contains more than 75,000 inhabitants, whose size and sudden growth are not less astonishing than that of the metropolis itself.

There are more people by several hundreds of thousands, within fifty miles of the central point of Manchester—which sits in the midst of the great towns of the north—than within the like distance of the central point of London.

In 1881 England and Wales had sixty per cent. of their entire population in towns and cities, and the rate of increase during the last two decades had been two and one-half times greater for the town than for the rural population.

No more striking illustration of the centralizing tendencies of modern times can be found than that which Scotland presents. The country parts of that land contain absolutely fewer people to-day than ten years ago; especially the Highlands. Timid deer are now the only inhabitants of many a grassy glen that used to furnish at the chieftain's summons its quota of a thousand men; wild forest creatures are sporting in hundreds of deserted cots, amid the brown and purple hills and beside the silver lochs, which were once merry with the shouts of children. Across the Highlands, a broad belt of beauty stretching from sea to sea, extend the hunting-grounds of the American millionaire, Mr. Winans; a modest little place for sport, comprising some eight hundred square miles. When land will bring ten times as great a rent for deer park as for agriculture or pasturage,* is it a wonder that the crofters have to leave their homes to the foxes? For every acre of mountain land employed in deer forest in 1840, there are at least ten in the present year. In this way the strength of nearly 2,000,000 acres, or 3,000 square miles of Scottish soil, are consumed to-day.† Meanwhile, Scotland has as many sons and daughters as ever. Her population has been steadily increasing since the beginning of the century, at the average rate of about eleven per cent. with each decade; but all this increase, and more than all, has poured itself into the cities. The country people are but a remnant. Three Scotchmen out of every four live in some city. The Glasgow among whose masses Chalmers labored with such power and effect contained only about 150,000 inhabitants. To-day, resounding with the roar of wheels and hammers, and dim in the smoke of countless chimneys, Glasgow strides on toward her million at a rate of increase which outstrips that of Chicago itself.‡ The laddies and lassies of song and fiction may still be tending sheep amid the mountain heather and making love in fields of rustling rye, but the laddies and lassies of fact are toiling in shops, factories, and noisy dock-yards, and when they meet and greet, it is by gaslight among the mighty throngs of Argyle Street and Trongate.

"While a few Scotchmen have castles and palaces, more than one-third of all Scottish families live in one

---

* J. Allanson Picton.   The Crofters Cry for More Land.   *Contem. Rev.*, Nov., 1885, p. 646.

† Mr. Cameron, of Lochiel.   A Defence of Deer Forests.   *Nineteenth Century*, Aug., 1885, p. 197.

‡ The increase of Glasgow between 1871 and 1881, amounted to 41.25 per cent. ; that of Chicago, to 40.78 per cent.

room each, and more than two-thirds in not more than two rooms each.* Thousands of acres are kept as a playground for strangers, while the masses have not enough of their native soil to grow a flower ; are shut out even from moor and mountain ; dare not take a trout from a loch or a salmon from a stream." †

Ireland exhibits the preference of the folk of modern times for city residences in the opposite way. For many years the Emerald Isle has been gradually losing her people, owing chiefly to the drainage of emigration, but it appears that for every two who have left the towns, ninety-eight have left her rural districts.

Cross the Channel, and in every European state which has felt the breath of the spirit of modern times, the same social tendencies are to be observed. On all sides cities are growing rapidly, while the population of country parts is growing very slowly—is at a standstill, or is even decreasing. Brussels has gained twenty per cent. and Antwerp thirty per cent., while Belgium, as a whole, has gained but eleven per cent. During the last decade, the rate of increase for the towns and cities in Denmark has been nearly twice as great as that for the rural districts. In Sweden it has been four times as great ; in Norway ten times as great. The four chief cities of Russia have doubled themselves within twenty years. The town population in Germany is growing about twice as rapidly as the whole population of the empire. The last census shows

---

* This statement, while literally true in 1870, was not quite true in 1880—the condition of things having in the meantime somewhat improved.

† Henry George. The Reduction to Iniquity. *Nineteenth Century,* July, 1884, p. 146.

that there are actually fewer people in the rural parts of Prussia than ten years ago, but the cities are greater by twenty-five per cent. In 1850 Berlin was a comparatively insignificant place, with some 400,000 inhabitants; she now ranks as third or fourth city in Christendom and boasts a population of 1,316,382. The same tendency is strikingly illustrated in France. For many years her population has been almost stationary, and, much of the time, even declining; yet, in the meantime, except for a brief period of interruption during the Franco-Prussian war, the French cities have steadily and rapidly increased in size and number. In 1846, out of every hundred Frenchmen, only twenty-four lived in the city; in 1861, there were twenty-nine; in 1881, thirty-four. Since the war, up to 1881, Paris added to her number fifty thousand souls for every year.* The same movement of the people might be noted in Austria, Italy, Switzerland, and Holland, as well as Canada and Australia. Nowhere is it more remarkably displayed than in our own country. It is not so surprising that men are crowded into the cities in Germany, which has 213 persons for every square mile of territory; or in England, which has 446; or in Belgium, which has 508. But cities increase in the same remarkable fashion in the United States, where we have less than 20 persons to the square mile, not including Alaska, and there are still scores of millions of acres to be given away.†

---

* Since 1881 her ratio of increase seems to nave been much slower. The growth of Paris and of all French and Italian cities is hindered by "octroi duties," or taxes on all provisions brought into the town; an arrangement which renders living much more costly within than outside the walls.

† In 1881, it was 17.29, or, including Alaska and Ind. Territory, 14.5 persons to the square mile.

The facts concerning the growth of American cities as reported by the census of 1880, have been widely circulated of late, especially in Dr. Strong's invaluable book;* but they will bear repeating. In 1790, one-thirtieth of our population lived in cities of eight thousand inhabitants and over. In 1800, the proportion of urban population had become one twenty-fifth; in 1820, it was one-twentieth; in 1830, one-sixteenth; in 1840, one-twelfth; in 1850, one-eighth; in 1860, one-sixth; in 1870, one-fifth; in 1880, nearly one-fourth, *i. e.*, 22.5 per cent.; from 1790 to 1880 the population of the country increased twelvefold, that of the cities eighty-six fold. In 1800, there were only six cities of over six thousand inhabitants; in 1880, there were two hundred and eighty-six.†

In the older States of the Union, the cities are draining the country in quite the European fashion. Hundreds of country towns in New England and New York have a population not half so numerous, and in other respects inferior, to what they had half a century ago. It is a common thing for the old farms to sell for less than the cost of the improvements on them. And yet so enormous is the increase of their great cities, that the Eastern States keep well abreast of the nation in its gigantic growth. Fifty-three out of every hundred inhabitants of Massachusetts reside in towns and cities, and two-thirds of these within twelve miles of the State House. As to the West, its cities springing up and growing great and splendid as it were in a night, are the marvel of the world. We be-

---

* Josiah Strong, D.D., *Our Country*, New York, 1886.
† See *Tenth Census of the United States*, vol. i., pp. xxviii. to xxx.

hold with wonder such places as Minneapolis, St. Paul, and Kansas City, towns that had not been heard of twenty years ago, selling their corner lots at Broadway prices.

A recent writer * has given a most ingenious illustration of the change in the distribution of men which the latter-day life has brought about. He calls attention to the fact that the area of England and Wales is nearly the same as that of New York and New Jersey ; that the population of England and Wales in 1688 was nearly the same as that of New York and New Jersey in 1870. You have, then, two districts of practically the same size, inhabited by the same number of people of the same blood and language. The one belongs to the seventeenth, the other to the nineteenth century. The district of the seventeenth century had for 5,500,000 people only five cities with a population greater than 10,000. The district of the nineteenth century has thirty-one such cities. Of the seventeenth century folk, less than one-fourth; of the nineteenth century folk, more than one half, are dwellers in great towns.

Such illustrations might be multiplied to any extent, but quite enough have been presented to establish the fact that during the present century a wonderful movement has passed over the face of the whole civilized world, suddenly shifting great sections of the people from the country to the towns, thereby changing the problems of life in manifold ways, and giving to the cities of the present, and still more promising to those of the future, a prominence in the world's affairs

---

* B. C. Magie, Jr. *Scribner's Magazine*, vol. xv.

hitherto unknown. Let us now examine the causes from which this movement has sprung.

That mysterious force named gravity, which gives to all bodies mutual tendencies toward each other, varying according to their masses, has a parallel in human society. A man, as a man, has a peculiar attractiveness to every other man. The attractive power of a group of men is greater than that of an individual; and the larger the group, the greater the mass of human life, the stronger is its influence in drawing outsiders to itself, and in holding those who have come to it.

As a race, we love not solitude; but there is built into us a fondness and a strong necessity for fellowship with our kind; for, since thought is awakened by thought alone, love by love, and passion by passion, the mind depends upon contact with other minds, not only for its exercise, growth, and enjoyment, but even for life. What food is to the body, that intercourse with other minds is to the mind of man, with the difference that the mental appetite is insatiable, and grows with feeding. There is, therefore, nothing more natural in the craving which drives the wild creature forth to its hunting-ground than in the social instinct which draws men into the currents and centres of life. This universal force of human attraction, like the force of gravitation, is, of course, frequently modified, and even nullified in its action by other forces. Race and family affinities bind one more firmly to his kith and kin than to the rest of men. Peculiarities of taste and temperament lead some to love solitude and hate society, and make certain sides of human nature particularly interesting to certain persons, and others distasteful. In some, the manhood is of a fuller, higher type than in others, and they are correspondingly more attractive ; while, from many, vice, poverty, and oppression have so beaten humanity out that little remains to invite the fellowship of men. Yet all these disturbing influences do not, on the whole, affect the operation of the great law, that man attracts man ; and that the greater the mass of humanity gathered about a centre. the more powerful upon the average outsider is the force of its attraction.

Every town and city is therefore a magnet constantly drawing the people from without toward itself, and binding together those within its walls with a power directly proportionate to its size. The magnetic influence of a great metropolis becomes so potent that multitudes find it too strong to be resisted. Thousands every year force their way into the midst of London, Paris, and New York, having no reasonable prospect of winning a livelihood, and insist upon staying there in miserable want rather than move out to more comfortable quarters elsewhere. The very vastness of the manifold life that throbs and thrills about them has a certain subtle fascination so intoxicating that they regard the idea of living in any lesser place as quite·insupportable. Juvenal shows that old Rome bewitched her populace by the same powerful spell. They used to pay for little, dark, wretched rooms a yearly rent great enough to have purchased a cheerful, comfortable dwelling in one of the lesser towns of Italy, but they could not be prevailed upon to leave the capital.*

---

* " If you can tear yourself away from the games in the circus, you can buy a capital house at Sara, or Fabratiria, or Frusino for the price at which you are now hiring your dark hole for one year." Juvenal, *Satir*, 166, 223, etc.

In the following passage, Charles Lamb, in his own charming way, gives voice to a sentiment that is far from being peculiar to himself; it is the sentiment of the multitudes :

"I have passed," says he, "all my days in London, until I have formed as many and as intense local attachments as any of your mountaineers can have done with dead nature. The lighted shops of the Strand and Fleet Street ; the innumerable trades, tradesmen, and customers, coaches, wagons, playhouses; all the bustle and wickedness round about Covent Garden; the watchmen, drunken scenes, rattles; life awake, if you awake, at all hours of the night, the impossibility of being dull in Fleet Street; the crowds, the very dirt and mud, the sun shining upon houses and pavements; the jewel shops, the old book stalls, parsons cheapening books, coffee-houses, steam of soup from kitchens, the pantomimes; London itself a pantomime and a masquerade,—all these things work themselves into my mind without a power of satiating me. The wonder of these sights impels me into night walks about her crowded streets, and I often shed tears in the motley Strand from fullness of joy at so much life." *

In a great city every man finds in its highest development the side and sort of life that pleases him best. For the vicious, there are unbounded opportunities for vice; for those who love God and men, extraordinary advantages for philanthropic work and Christian fellowship. Many, with special musical, literary, or artistic talents, are quite alone in a small community with neither opportunity nor stimulus for growth in the di-

---

* Charles Lamb, *Letter to Wordsworth.*

rections toward which their tastes incline them; but upon entering a city they find the surroundings so congenial that they can never again be persuaded to quit them. With its libraries, lectures, public gatherings, book-stores, companionships, and above all, the perpetual stimulus of contact with many minds, the great city is the paradise of literary men. Hume pronounced it the only fit place of residence for a man of letters. Dr. Johnson declared that a man who was tired of London was tired of his own existence. " Sir," said the great man as he sat in Mitre Tavern beside Temple Bar, " the happiness of London is not to be conceived but by those who have been in it. I will venture to say, there is more learning and science within the circumference of ten miles from where we sit than in all the rest of the kingdom." Dr. Chalmers, in comparing the country with the city pastorate, remarks, that while the latter lacks leisure, the former lacks stimulus, and that for the highest achievements stimulus is of far greater importance than leisure. In the same strain are Mr. Emerson's words: " A scholar is a candle which the love and desire of all men will light."

Great cities have a special fascination for young men. They offer to the successful, high and tempting prizes. There is little in the position of leading merchant, lawyer, or physician in a country town to spur the ambition of the young; but those who hold the like positions in the cities are the princes and mighty men of the times. Ambitious fellows prefer a hard race with high stakes to one on an easier course with fewer competitors and contemptible prizes. Hence, they have flocked to the cities until a new attorney's sign has become a by-word, and a single advertisement for a book-keeper enough to bring an army about your door. Besides all these special attractions for special classes, who can measure the fascination for the masses of manhood, of the great city's unequalled facilities for instruction and amusement? The churches and the schools, the theatres and concerts, the lectures, fairs, exhibitions, and galleries—how widely on every side are the doors of life opened! Even the streets and the shops have an attraction that few can deny ; the bright and costly goods displayed in the windows, the prancing horses and sparkling carriages, the roar and rumble of drays, wagons, and cars, and the mighty streams of human beings that forever flow up and down the thoroughfares, exhibiting such an infinite variety of face, feature, form, and dress, from exquisite beauty to hideous ugliness, and from the richest silks and furs to the filthiest, faded, fluttering rags. But above and beyond all this is that vague delight at being one in the midst of a great multitude of men and women, which, though it may not often be defined or expressed, is the greatest of all the causes which contribute to the cities' growth.

Such tendencies would draw the whole world into cities,—into one great city, perhaps,—were it not for the existence of certain opposite tendencies—centrifugal forces, as one may call them—which counterbalance the centripetal force and preserve the equilibrium of society. While, on the one hand, city life is richer than rural, on the other it is more costly and less healthful. It is more costly because food, fuel, and every needful product of the soil must be produced by others, and brought from afar; because competition for the land is great and rent high; because the cost of living being great, personal service is correspondingly costly. City

3

life is less healthful than the rural, because of the difficulty in getting a good and sufficient supply of the four things on which life chiefly depends: food, water, air, and light. Many must go with an insufficient quantity of food because of its costliness; and that they have, being the cheapest, is often unwholesome. Water is difficult to get, and unless brought from afar at great expense, is almost sure to be tainted with impurity. In closely crowded quarters filth quickly accumulates, and cleanliness can only be secured by eternal vigilance. No art has been discovered by which the air of a great town can be kept free from the disease germs and poisonous gases that reek from noisome places. Where thousands of furnaces are pouring their foul breath out into the sky, and where hundreds of thousands of human beings are always robbing the air of its vitality, a far less wholesome atmosphere necessarily prevails than on the mountain-side or by the sea; sickness comes on more easily and is harder to throw off. All these difficulties obviously bear most heavily upon the poorer classes. The tattered fringe which hangs upon the border of the social fabric is broadest in cities. That portion of the people, comprising the poorest, the weakest, and the most helpless, which is being gradually crowded to the wall and crushed amid the strife and struggle of the strong, is found largely—in some countries almost wholly—in the towns.

Such, then, are the practical checks upon the growth of cities. They can increase no faster than the costliness of living and wholesomeness of life within their walls allow. The great cities of antiquity were always so situated that they could obtain a plenty of cheap food. Rome was able to rival the populousness of

modern capitals because she had peculiar advantages
for feeding the multitude. She was rich. The treas-
ures of the whole earth flowed into her lap. She could
afford to buy the best from all the markets in the world.
The great food-producing countries were close at hand,
clustered about the Mediterranean, in the midst of
which she sat, accessible on every side by land and sea.
Bread was cheap in Rome : sometimes, even, it was
free to the poor. Nor was the vastness of the population which she found it possible to sustain, less due
to the fact that she was able to make life supportable
and even healthful within her walls. The system of
aqueducts, sewers, and public baths, by which she
secured to her citizens good sanitary conditions, have
never since been approached in magnificence, costliness, and efficiency.*

The following may, therefore, be laid down as the
law of the growth of cities. The urban population in
every country is always as large as its circumstances
allow. When a city's increase is not checked by the
superior attractiveness of some rival, it will grow until
it reaches a point where life within its walls becomes
so difficult because of extreme costliness or unwhole-
someness, or both, that it is no longer to be preferred
to life without.

If we now turn our attention toward London again,
and follow its lines back into the past, we shall see
abundant evidence that at every step of its history the
population has been as great as could be sustained

---

* Rome still enjoys from ancient aqueducts the most abundant
water supply of any great city in the world. Until within a few
years the saying was literally true that one could not go away from
the sound of running water in Rome.

under existing circumstances, with a continual tendency
to overstep the limits of possible crowding, a trans-
gression followed by great misery, hunger, and disease,
which at frequent intervals broke out into violent forms
of plague and famine.

Famines used to be among the regular features of
London life in the olden time. They were often accompanied by a degree of distress for which we, in
our day, have no parallel. We read, for example, of a
great famine brought on by a wet season in the year
1257, when 20,000 people starved to death in London.
Only thirteen years later there came another still more
dreadful dearth. "Wheat sold at six pounds eight
shillings the quarter (which is more than sixty pounds
at present). And the famine was so horrible that
parents are reported to have eaten their own children."*
The reasons for the latter dearth are thus explained :
"By excessive rains, the banks of the Thames over-
flowed and broke down in many places, by which accident immense injury was done to houses, lands, and
fruits of the earth." It is, at first sight, incredible that
a mere wet season should ever have occasioned the
starvation of every seventh man in London, or that a
freshet of the Thames should have driven the famish-
ing poor in the frenzy of hunger to the point of devour-
ing their own offspring. Yet it must be remembered
that in those days London had almost no food except
what grew in the fields immediately about her. When
these failed to yield their harvest, starvation was at
hand. Four hundred years later it was still true that
the hay, straw, peas, beans, and oats used in London

---

* Noorthouck's *History of London*, pp. 50 and 56. London, 1773.

were principally raised within a circuit of twenty miles
of the metropolis. The extreme difficulty of bringing
food from the interior, will be seen at once when it is
remembered that everything had to be carried on pack-
horses over roads so narrow that two could not go
abreast on one of them, and incredibly rough and
difficult.* A curious light is thrown upon the condition of the old English roads by the recorded fact
that during the civil war eight hundred horses were
captured while sticking in the mud. Only a century
ago, the cost of freight between London and Birming-
ham was £5 per ton, having fallen less than £2 per ton
in a hundred years. At the same time, the rate between
London and Leeds was £13 per ton.†

The history of the great city on the Thames records a
long series of efforts, dating back to the earliest time,
aimed at making bread cheap by legislation. We read,
for example, that in the year 1314 provisions of all
sorts were so excessively dear that Parliament imposed
a regular price upon every variety of flesh and fowl. But
instead of relieving the difficulties of the citizens, this
measure increased their distress ; for its immediate
effect was to cut off the supply of provisions altogether,
so that it was shortly afterward repealed. " Indeed,"
says the historian, " although it is often wished for in
our time, it does not appear possible to limit the price
of provisions by any law or magistracy without doing
more harm than good." ‡ It is instructive to notice the
extreme fluctuation in the cost of provisions in Lon-

---

* See Smiles' *Lives of the Engineers*, vol. i., p. 177. London, 1861.

† *A History of Ireland Navigation*, p. 73. London, 1769.

‡ Noorthouck, p. 63.

don. The price of wheat would frequently be twice as great one winter as the next. In times of famine it would rise to incredible figures. All this meant a hard and doubtful fight for life on the part of the humbler class of citizens.

But the sufferings of London from pestilence have been even greater than those from famine. It took her centuries to learn the simplest laws of health. Her water supply used to be drawn from wells in the city, which were, of course, defiled by impurities ; and even when she introduced water-works, the water was pumped up from the river by tide-wheels at London Bridge, where it was anything but pure. There was no sewerage worthy of the name ; the streets were not paved until the seventeenth century, and filth was allowed to accumulate in them until, in many portions, they were higher than the ground floor of the houses, from whose lower rooms the drippings of the roadway were with difficulty excluded.* Under such circumstances, it is no wonder that the death-rate was always fearfully heavy, and that epidemics of disease frequently prevailed.

Small-pox was an inveterate enemy of the London folk. It used to destroy, upon an average, one life out of every seven.† There was also a dreadful sweating sickness, as it was called, which visited London repeat-

---

* Erasmus gives a shocking picture of the ordinary artisan's habitation in his time. "They were filthy beyond description. The floors were of loam strewed with rushes, which were constantly put on fresh without the removal of the old, and intermixed with bones, broken victuals, and dirt." Quoted by Loftie, *History of London*, vol. i., p. 354. London, 1883.

† Noorthouck, p. 136, note.

edly in the sixteenth century and destroyed thousands
of people. But the worst of all was that loathsome
and terrible disease called "the plague," which every
few years stole upon the unfortunate city like some
savage monster creeping up out of the deep, and
snatched away thousands of her children. In the
seventeenth century London alone was afflicted by no
less than four visitations of this dread pestilence.* On
the first occasion, six thousand citizens perished; on
the second, above thirty-five thousand victims were
swept away. There were eight deaths to one birth in
London that year. Only eleven years later ten thousand more were carried off by some foe, and, in the
memorable year 1665, the great plague, like the horror
of a great darkness, settled down upon London and
smote the people until her crowded homes were empty,
her bustling streets and busy marts desolate, and the
number of the living seemed less than they that were
dead. "Most terrible stories of premature burial were
circulated. All business was suspended; grass grew
in the streets; no one went about; the rumbling wheels
of the cart and the cry, 'Bring out your dead,' alone
broke the stillness of the night."† Although one-third
of the people with the king and court fled from the
doomed city, the deaths increased daily until they
reached the rate of fifteen hundred a day. Bills of
mortality recorded as many as 68,596 deaths from the
plague that year, but in the terror and confusion of the
darkest days no complete record could be kept, and
historians agree that these figures represent only a
fraction of the multitude swept away in the carnival of

---

* See Loftie, vol. i., p. 353.   † Loftie, vol. i., p. 357.

death. In the following year came the great fire of
London, in whose fierce and fearful flames the town
was so purified that it suffered no more from the
plague during that century.

So great was the hindrance to the city's growth
caused by want and disease breaking out from time to
time in these violent forms, that up to the beginning
of the present century, it does not seem to have increased, on the average, more than fifty per cent. each
century, or, at the exceedingly slow rate of one-half of
one per cent. a year. Yet even that rate appeared too
rapid. Queen Elizabeth issued two proclamations in
which the inhabitants of London were forbidden to
erect new buildings where none had existed before
within the memory of man. It was said that extension
of the metropolis would encourage the increase of the
plague; would create trouble in governing such multitudes; would cause a dearth of victuals, a multiplying
of beggars and inability to relieve them, and an increase of artisans more than could live together.

The decree further stated that lack of air and room
to walk or shoot arose out of too crowded a city.
James I. issued several proclamations to the same intent. "We do well perceive," says he, "in Our Princely
wisdom and prudence, now that Our Citie of London
is become the greatest, or next the greatest Citie of the
Christian World, it is more than time that there bee an
utter cessation of further New Building." One among
the stained and yellow documents which bear this
monarch's name is of special interest in this connection.
It is that in which "On account of the present scarcity
and dearth, and of the high prices of corn and grain,"
he commands all lords (spiritual and temporal), knights,

and gentlemen of quality who are staying in or near the city of London to return at once to their country seats. He also commands the magistrates to compel all farmers to bring forth what grain they have in store and to sell the same at reasonable prices. Charles I., by repeated proclamations, forbade any building of any sort whatever on new foundations within three miles of any of the gates of London or of the palace at Westminster. He also prohibited the subdivision of any building into tenements, more than at present or for thirty years past, and the receiving of more families than one into a single tenement. A similar proclamation was issued to prevent new building and overcrowding in Edinburgh. Cromwell issued proclamations to the same intent; and, after the restoration, we find Charles II. repeating, in similar terms, the prohibition of his father and grandfather and giving the same reasons therefor.*

Thus it appears that the London of the past has been quite as monstrous, quite as unmanageable, quite as full of the poor, the sickly, and the starving, as the London of the present, and when her actual population was not one-tenth of what it is, she was overcrowded even more than now. Had we time to examine the history of the people of Paris, Vienna, or Edinburgh, or any other of the older important cities of Europe, we should see the same thing. Until recent times, their increase has been continually checked and prevented by the battle with hunger and the ravages of disease as well as by arbitrary enactments.

---

* These proclamations are still preserved in the Library of the British Museum.

During the latter part of the eighteenth century, a new day in the world's history began to dawn,—the era of what has been termed "modern civilization." It was then that men first commenced in any considerable degree to reinforce themselves by "borrowing the might of the elements." The steam-engine had been partially invented for a century or more, but had been used only for pumping and as a scientific toy. James Watt made it of practical value and set it to work. In 1788 it was for the first time successfully harnessed to the wheels of a mill.* Close upon this, followed that long series of mechanical inventions which have made steam power serviceable in such an infinite variety of ways, revolutionizing the whole system of human industry. In the discovery of the steam-engine, the mother of machines, may be found the central reason for the growth of our nineteenth-century cities.

This resulted, in the first place, from the increment that the steam-engine brought to the world's wealth. Work is the source of wealth. All work had hitherto been done and all wealth won by tedious process of manual labor; but here was a contrivance for converting heat into work. There was heat enough to be had; stored up in latent form, the bowels of the earth were black with it. The great invention, therefore, changing in magical fashion the cheap and grimy product of the mines into work and into wealth, was like a veritable philosopher's stone dropped down into the midst of the nations. What the fathers had gained slowly with hard toil and sweat of the face, the sons gained swiftly

---

* Albion Mill in London. See Smiles' *Lives of the Engineers*, vol. ii.

by the aid of steam, fierce furnaces bearing the heat, and sinews of steel, the burden of the day.

It is difficult to realize how rapidly the world has been growing rich during the present century. Mr. Gladstone estimates that the amount of wealth which could be handed down to posterity, produced during the first eighteen hundred years of the Christian era, was equalled by the production of the first fifty years of this century, and that an equal amount was produced in the twenty-five years from 1850 to 1875.* No doubt as much more has been produced since 1875, if, as he further estimates, the manufacturing power of the world is doubled by the aid of machinery every seven years. Mr. Mulhall, by carefully arranged statistics, has not only shown that the Queen's subjects are worth on the average some $335 apiece more than they were thirty years ago, and, excluding Ireland, nearly twice as much as they were in Queen Anne's time, due allowance being made for the difference in the purchasing power of money,—but he has also exhibited the fact, that as England's wealth has increased, its distribution among the people has become more general † As for our own country, the last census informs us that between 1860 and 1880, the wealth of the United States increased three times as fast as its population, notwithstanding the waste of the war and the extinguishment of vast property by the liberation of the slaves.

The immediate result of such increase of wealth has been an extremely rapid growth of the world's popula-

---

* Quoted in *Our Country*, p. 115.

† Paper on *The Increase of the National Wealth since the Time of the Stuarts*, read at the British Association, September 24, 1883.

tion. Within a lifetime, the inhabitants of the civilized world have doubled in number, and the number of those who speak the English language has quadrupled.

After the Norman Conquest it took England six hundred years to add three millions to her population. She has done more than that within the last ten years. That this great and sudden growth has been caused by the general increase of the world's wealth may be seen from the fact that it is due, not so much to an increase of the birth-rate, as to a decrease of the death-rate among civilized peoples. The average span of a human life in England, Germany, and France is now six years longer than it was when Victoria ascended the throne, and is still increasing.* Men are healthier and live longer, because they are able to afford more and better food; more and better clothing; better homes, and superior sanitary and domestic arrangements.

A secondary result of the increase in the world's wealth has been an increase in the size of the cities. The greater supply of wealth means not only more people, but more rich people; people, a greater proportion of whom can afford to pay the high rents, and buy the costly provisions of the towns. The increase of wealth caused by machinery thus builds up cities in two ways at once: it increases the whole number of inhabitants in the land, and, at the same time, the proportion of those inhabitants who can afford a town residence.

Increased wealth has increased the safety and salubriousness of the cities, thus making them more desirable places of residence. Drains, sewers, water-works,

---

* Michael G. Mulhall, *Progress of the World*, p. 6. London, 1880.

street-cleaning and other sanitary arrangements, have
worked wonders in our towns during the last few decades. The death-rate is continually falling. The plague
of the middle ages is known no more; even the cholera,
which was so destructive twenty and thirty years ago,
does not easily get a foothold of late. But all these
sanitary arrangements are exceedingly costly, and are
only possible where there is great wealth.

The charities which the wealth of modern times sustains have also an important social influence. Nature
provides for the disadvantages that the poor suffer in
comparison with the well-to-do, in the struggle for existence, in her wonted way, viz : by giving to the poor
a larger number of children in view of the probability
that a greater proportion of those children will succumb
to disease and privation before reaching maturity;*
but as a city grows in wealth, and its donations for
charitable purposes increase, increasing numbers of
those who would otherwise perish in early life are
rescued from the clutches of want and sickness. The
free hospitals, infirmaries, homes for destitute children,
etc., with their superior medical service, care and nursing must have vast influence in diminishing the power
of poverty and disease to check the natural increase of
population. It is estimated that £4,000,000 is given
away in London every year, the greater part of which
is expended for benevolent purposes within its limits,
and that the charitable work of the hospitals alone in-
volves an annual expenditure of above £500,000. Such

---

* Between 1870 and 1880 the birth-rate in the prosperous district
of Hampstead, London, was twenty-four per thousand annually,
whereas, in the miserable district of White Chapel it was thirty-six
per thousand, or fifty per cent. greater.

institutions unquestionably save multitudes of lives, and their work goes far toward explaining the fact that eighty-one per cent. of the annual increase of that city is due to the excess of its birth-rate over its death-rate, while the influx from the rural districts, from other towns and from foreign lands, altogether amounts to less than nineteen per cent. of the whole increase.

By another most important agency has the steam-engine promoted the growth of cities: that is the railroad. The country lad no longer comes trudging into town dusty and footsore, with a bundle on his back, a few shillings in his pocket, and the alternative before him of finding a place or starving. The farmer's boy who goes into the city seeking a situation at present runs no risk. If he fails to find it, he can easily take the next train for home, and try again some other day. Thus the iron road enables the town to make its attractiveness far more widely felt than formerly. It also greatly increases the convenience of getting about from suburb to centre, and from one part of town to another. Men can live at greater distances from their business, and the cities can hold more inhabitants with less crowding. But the greatest service that the railways render to the cities is that of facilitating the arrangements by which they are fed. Two hundred years ago, London, like a frugal household of the olden time, used to lay up a supply of food in autumn sufficient for the whole winter's needs, the greater part of which came from the immediate neighborhood. Now it is said that she never has more than a week's supply on hand, and that a fortnight's siege would bring her to starvation. Then, the cost of food was great and irregular, the supply uncertain, periods of dearth frequent, and famines occasional. Now, the price of provisions is uniform, is much less than then, the supply is regular, and famine impossible. Forty years ago, Mr. Porter, the best economist in England, said: " Great Britain can never obtain the bulk of her food supply from abroad, as all the shipping in the world, say 6,600,000 tons, would be insufficient to carry food for her population." To-day, Great Britain imports more than half her food, and employs in doing so ships whose tonnage exceeds that of the world's shipping when Mr. Porter wrote.* Forty years ago the price of grain in Western Prussia was double that which ruled in Eastern Prussia. Forty years ago the cost of wheat was 150 per cent. higher in England than in Hungary; the present difference in price is only 23 per cent. In half a century the price of wheat has fallen thirty-five per cent. in England, and the consumption has risen, per inhabitant, thirty-two per cent.† The significance of such changes will be seen when it is remembered that the death-rate, as shown by Doctor Farr, of the Statistical Society, rises and falls in England with the price of bread. In the opinion of experts, railroads have also operated very powerfully in favor of the great towns at the expense of the small ones, especially in the United States, by the discrimination in freight rates against the latter. The charges for shipping goods from a little town have frequently been twice as great as from a city, where two or more lines compete for the traffic. This, of course, makes it difficult for manufacturers and traders to locate in a small community.

---

* Mulhall, pp. 133 and 134.

† Andrew Carnegie states that one dollar will ship as much freight across the Atlantic to-day as thirty-five dollars twenty years ago.

The steam-engine and the wealth produced by it and by machinery have contributed to the growth of cities in another way : they have increased the demand for such products as come from the towns, and have, therefore, multiplied the opportunities of earning a livelihood within them.   There is a principle well known to economists called "Engel's Law," the essence of which is this : As the income increases, the relative percentage of outlay for food, the great product of the country, diminishes, while the relative percentage of outlay for sundries,—that is, the various manufactured articles or products of the town,—becomes greater. As men grow richer, a larger part of their wants must be supplied by labor in the factories, and a smaller proportion by labor in the fields; therefore, the richer the world, the greater will naturally be the proportion of its people who work within brick walls and walk on crowded pavements.

Again; under the new conditions consequent upon the introduction of the steam-engine the volume of the world's trade has marvelously increased.   With vastly more wealth to be expended and invested than formerly, with an infinite quantity and variety of articles to be bought and sold, many of which had never been heard of fifty years ago, with rapid transit and cheap freight so that the remotest parts can send their products to market for exchange, with multitudes of new facilities for the conduct of trade, better methods of banking, telegraphic communication, mails, expresses, etc., the nineteenth century has witnessed a revolution of commerce second only to that of manufacture, and one that has been almost equally powerful in its tendency to build up the cities.   The city has always been the home of trade, the place of shops and shoppers, of markets and merchandise, so that under any circumstances the growth of a nation's trade would involve a corresponding increase of its towns ; but this has been peculiarly the case in recent years, because the growth of trade has been accompanied by constant improvements in the facilities for intercommunication. The city shops serve a wider circle of country customers every day. You can live in Texas in these times and do your shopping in New York.

There is still another cause for the enormous development of the cities which is of great importance, namely : the change in methods of agricultural work. This reason is not so immediately connected with the steam-engine, although it is the outcome of that series of inventions to which the discovery of the steam-engine gave the first impulse. With each successive year, a smaller and smaller proportion of the world's workers are required to produce the world's food. What ten men used to do with difficulty, one man now does with ease through the aid of machinery. "It is a fact, estimated by careful men thoroughly conversant with the changes that have taken place, that by the improvement made in agricultural tools the average farmer can, with sufficient horse-power, do with three men the work of fourteen men forty years ago, and do it better." * This fact has a twofold influence in increasing the urban population: it pulls and it pushes at once; it expels men from the country, it attracts them to the towns.

A farmer buys such improved machines as enable him to dispense with the services, say, of two laborers.

---

* Report of Special Agent on Agricultural Implements, *Tenth Census U. S.*, vol. ii., p. 700.

His farm yields as large crops as ever, but two farm-hands less are required to do the work. These two men, being thrust out of employment by the machine, are compelled to seek it elsewhere; and by this number with their families, the region of the farm is depopulated. Meanwhile, the amount which the farmer formerly expended for the wages of the dismissed laborers is added to his income, but he does not keep much of this money. A part of it goes in payment for the new machines, and a part of it for the purchase of such luxuries as could not be afforded before,—better clothing, furniture, books, etc.,—all of which come from the cities, and consequently involve additional labor for city manufacturers and traders. Thus while the result of the new machine is to diminish the demand for labor in the country, it increases the demand for labor in town; and the men thrown out of work on the farm, will naturally find it in shop or factory. The proportion of laborers in the United States who are engaged in agriculture as compared with the proportion of laborers engaged in manufacture and other occupations shows a remarkable diminution between 1870 and 1880.* Says Mr. Alfred Simmons, Secretary of the Kent and Sussex Laborer's Union: "I am personally acquainted with many parishes, the land on which formerly provided regular employment for from two hundred to three hundred laborers, but on which there are now employed not one-half the original number, and many of those so employed only casually engaged. In every department of agriculture, the machine has taken the best paid for agricultural work from the laborer."†

---

* *Tenth Census U. S.*, vol. i., p. 703.

† Pamphlet entitled *State Emigration ; a reply to Lord Derby.* Pub-

"One farmer, like Dr. Glyn, of California, or Mr. Dalrymple, of Dakota, with a field of wheat covering a hundred square miles, can raise as much grain with four hundred farm servants as five thousand peasant proprietors in France." *

"The plowshare may be silver, but the spade is gold," say the Italians. Modern agriculturists have proved the saying false. Not only do the machines do more work than the hand-tools, but they do it better. In the days of Queen Anne, the wheat-fields of England used to yield fifteen bushels to the acre. The little peasant farms of France and Germany yield about the same amount now.† To-day, with large fields and improved agricultural methods, the average yield for the United Kingdoms is thirty-six bushels per acre.‡

With each successive year the production of a barrel of flour, a bushel of corn or potatoes, or a round of beef, requires less labor.

With each successive year a smaller part of the world's ever-increasing army of workers can be employed in the ordinary pursuits of agriculture. But the law of life, "in the sweat of thy face shalt thou eat bread," has lost none of the rigor of its enforcement. Men toil as long and hard for daily bread in

---

lished by the National Society for Promoting State-directed Emigration and Colonization.

* See Mulhall's *Progress of the World*, pp. 23 and 24.

† Lady Verney, "Foreign Opinions on Peasant Properties." *Nineteenth Century*, Nov., 1885, p. 796.

‡ In France and Germany, where the old methods of hand-labor largely prevail, each male person employed produces on an average, respectively, only 220 and 245 bushels of wheat each year. In England, where the modern methods prevail, the average product of every person is 540 bushels. In the United States it is 820 bushels.

this year of grace as they did before mowing, reaping, and threshing-machines appeared ; but the bulk of the work has been changed from field to factory and the majority of the workers have followed it.

Such reasons as these afford abundant explanation for the phenomenal increase of urban populations in modern times. Civilization has promoted the growth of the great towns by augmenting their natural attractiveness, the facilities for reaching them and the opportunities of earning a livelihood with them, and, at the same time, by decreasing the obstacles and broadening the natural limits to their growth. It has brought to them an unlimited supply of cheap food, greater wealth to meet the costliness of city residence, and to overcome by proper sanitary arrangements the unhealthfulness of their crowded life. And, finally, it has been continually changing the balance of the demand for work and workers, from the country to the town.

So long as such causes as these prevail, the cities of Christendom will continue rolling themselves up to ever vaster size ; but these causes as yet show no diminution in their influence ; nor, so far as one may judge, are they likely to do so for generations to come.* The present may be the age of great cities, but the future is the age of greater. This must especially be the case with the United States. The youngest of the nations has already more large cities than any except Great Britain and Germany. Though still in their infancy,

---

* If it could be shown that poverty and crime were increasing more rapidly than population in the larger cities, there would be an indication that they were approaching the limit of possible growth under the present conditions of civilization. As a matter of fact, however, official returns for England, Scotland, and Germany show an opposite tendency.

our principal towns surpass in size and in the tumult of their life, many of the older and flourishing capitals of Europe. With the country growing in population at a rate unprecedented in the annals of all times and the towns growing twice as fast; with what seems a certainty of having as many inhabitants within one hundred years as all Europe has at present; with every probability that the people of the twentieth century will centralize themselves even more than those of the nineteenth, the United States may fairly expect to possess cities whose greatness cannot be equalled by anything that the world has yet seen.

All efforts to arrest the progress of the cities and to check the population that continually flows into them, must be fruitless. The great social movements of the age cannot be stopped Each successive year is certain to see a smaller place for the workers of the world in the fields and on the farms and a larger place in shops, counting-rooms, offices, banks, manufactories, and the myriad industries that make their home in the metropolis. Let it not be assumed that great cities are of necessity, what Thomas Jefferson called them : "Great sores upon the body ploitic." Nothing is evil that is in the best sense natural, and the formation of great cities is a normal result of a high development of human society. They are found among the purest and most advanced of nations ; they come in the most enlightened times ; the evil of them is not in their size, but in the avarice, luxury, oppression, and vice that haunt them.

The wisest efforts of philanthropy will not be spent in the vain effort to prevent the incoming of men to them, but in the effort to make them better places for human habitation ; not in checking their growth, but in quenching their iniquity.

CHAPTER II.

FEW thoughtful men can look attentively upon the tumultuous life of a great town, traverse the monotonous miles of its extensive suburbs, or mingle in the human tides that flow forever up and down its thoroughfares, without the repeated question: Who are all these people? whence came they? how do they live?

The inhabitants of cities may be classified by their occupation. Most men have something to do; notwithstanding a prevailing impression to the contrary, the census returns show that the number of able-bodied male adults who have no regular profession, occupation, or calling, is exceedingly small. In all England and Wales it amounts to but 186,000, and in our own land it must be much less, seeing that we have no professional gentry.

Cities have three kinds of work: production, distribution, service. There are, therefore, three sorts of workers: those employed in making goods, those employed in selling and distributing goods, and those who tender to others their professional or personal services *

The work of production is the great business of cities, a business which employs more workers than either distribution or service, and often more than both

---

* The data for the following discussion are found in the *Tenth Census of the United States*, vol. i., pp. 700-900.

combined. This is especially true in the United States.
We have risen, within the past twenty years, to the
first place among the manufacturing nations of the
world and manufacture has been the life of our towns.
Our trade, vast as its volume is, has done less to swell
the cities than the manufactures that centre in them.
"I conceive," says Francis A. Walker, "that no one
will hesitate to assent to the proposition that the growth
of the cities of the United States since 1850, has been
due in far greater measure to their development as
manufacturing centres than to their increased business
as centres for the distribution of commercial products." *
Even in the great trade cities, such as New York,
Boston, anel Chicago, there are more persons engaged
in making goods than in selling them † In the fifty
chief cities the ratio of producers to distributors is that
of 13 to 7, a very great proportion then,—and often
the majority of those who people the long lines of
houses, who throng the streets, who consume the stores
of provisions, who make the money and spend the
money, who swell the census tables, and, in a word,
constitute the population of the ordinary American
city, get their living by some sort of manufacture or
mechanical work.

A few of those thus employed are manufacturers and
officials and clerks of manufacturing companies ; a few
are master mechanics, contractors, and other employers
of labor; but at least nine-tenths are artisans. These
artisans are nearly all dependent for work and for

---

* Remarks on the Statistics of Manufacture. *Tenth Census of the
United States*, vol. ii., pp. xv. and xvi.

† Kansas City is the only exception noticed.

wages upon employers and belong to what is called "the working-class." The independent mechanic who works by himself at his home or in a small shop with one or two apprentices as assistants, is rarely to be found in our modern towns. "Of the nearly 3,000,000 people employed in the mechanical industries in this country," says Mr. Carroll D. Wright, the best of authorities, "at least four-fifths are working under the factory system." *
Among the rest, most of whom, from the nature of their occupation, cannot be working in factories, such as carpenters, plumbers, painters, paper-hangers, and masons, the majority are working for day wages under the employ of large builders and contractors.

In production of every sort, two tendencies are noteworthy. The first is, the incessant substitution of unskilled labor for skilled through the aid of machinery. So ingenious are the contrivances of modern mechanics that children and untaught persons take the places and do the work of those who have learned their craft by long apprenticeship. The quantity of brain work requisite in the ordinary mechanic is daily diminishing; so is the quantity of sheer physical strength. Mere deftness of hand or nimbleness of fingers is the only quality now necessary for the production of many an article which once cost skill and patience of the highest quality, as well as muscle. This means that the common artisan of the machinery age takes less and less thoughtful interest in his work and requires less and less intelligence and strength as improvements in machines and engines continue.

---

* Special report on "Factories and the Factory System." *Tenth Census of the United States*, vol. ii., p. 548.

Another notable tendency of modern industry is toward the concentration of manufacture in large establishments. A large concern has every advantage over a small one: more capital, more independence, better machines, less waste, better facilities for buying and selling. The two cannot compete on equal terms. The small establishments must either devote themselves to some specialty where they have the field to themselves, must consolidate, or must entirely break up In Massachusetts, for example, the annual industrial products are three and one-half times greater than they were thirty-five years ago, and those employed in their pro duction twice as many; yet the number of manufacturing establishments has increased only sixty-eight per cent. since 1850. This means larger establishments and less of them, fewer employers and more employés; this means that with every year more men are working for wages and less men are engaged in enterprises of their own. So long as industrial tendencies continue as they are, factory-people and wage-working artisans, in whose work there is so little to stimulate either intellectual or physical development, must compose a large and a somewhat increasing proportion of the inhabitants of all cities.

The second great branch of industry is that of distribution. Under this head are included all bankers, brokers, insurance agents, merchants, and dealers of every sort, as well as the army of salesmen, clerks, accountants, packers, and porters employed by them; and, at the same time, all those connected with railways, street-cars, express lines, cabs, drays, freight and shipping offices. Though not so numerous as those engaged in manufacture and mechanical industries, this class composes a large and very important portion of urban society.

To it belongs the great bulk of the wealth, and a large share of the power and influence. Merchant princes and railroad kings may be few, but merchants of independent position and comfortable income are numerous; and still more numerous are the small dealers and the clerks, agents, and salesmen of various sorts who live on respectable salaries. These are the people that swell the ranks of what in England are called the " middle classes," that crowd the shops and fill the better streets, that attend the churches, concerts, and respectable theatres. They are, withal, so much the most conspicuous part of the city's population that they appear to constitute a larger portion of the whole than they do in reality. Yet the number of workingmen employed in distribution, especially in connection with railroads and transportation, is at the same time very considerable, so that in this branch of industry as well as that of production, a greater part of those engaged are in humble circumstances.

The third class of occupations comprises all that make it their business to contribute any kind of professional or personal service to other men. A very wide range of employments is included under this head. Commencing with the so-called " professional classes,"— lawyers, clergymen, physicians, journalists, teachers, and Government officers—the list is extended through hotel-keepers, keepers of stables, laundries, barber-shops, and boarding-houses, and finally, includes domestic servants and simple unspecified day-laborers. This class, if not so numerous as either of the other two, is by no means a small one.* It is made up for

---

* In order to make a fair comparison, one must compare the males of each class.

the most part, though perhaps not so largely as the manufacturers, of those who work with the hands for daily wages. Some who hold the highest and most influential positions are, indeed, included here, but such persons compose a very slight numerical portion of the whole.*

This hasty glance at the occupations of the people makes it evident that in all three branches of industry the workers are divided into two classes, according as the chief element in their work is that of brain or muscle. Workers of the one class are engaged in "business," those of the other in "labor." The rewards of the first are "profits," "fees," or "salaries." Those of the second are "wages." People of the first class are never, except by blustering anarchists, called "idle men," but those of the second are generally distinguished by the noble title, "workingmen," a designation which, much as we disapprove of it when so employed, we cannot well avoid the use of. The income of the first class is much greater, their style of living better, their homes more comfortable, and their food more wholesome and abundant; they have better opportunities for the improvement of the mind and the culture of the taste, and are, consequently, as a class, more thoughtful, intelligent, and better informed. The boundary line between workingmen and others is not sharply drawn; some who work for wages are far

---

* Under this head, for instance, the census shows that there are in New York for 800 journalists, 3,700 barbers; less than 900 clergymen, more than 9,000 launderers and laundresses; 2,600 physicians and surgeons, more than 12,000 hotel and restaurant employés; 3,000 lawyers, 35,000 laborers; less than 5,000 teachers, more than 55,000 domestic servants.

superior in intelligence and social standing to the average of those who work for salaries. Nevertheless, the term "workingman" conveys a distinct notion of that great portion of society that bears the physical burdens and performs the bone-and-muscle labor, that carries the heaviest loads and receives the smallest rewards.

It is also evident that the great bulk of the population in ordinary cities must be composed of the working-class, since they comprise not less than four-fifths of those engaged in productive industries, one-third of those engaged in distribution and three-fourths of those engaged in service. The proportion of workingmen to others in a given town, would, of course, depend greatly upon the character of its leading industries. You would expect to find a much larger percentage of wage-workers in a city of great mills, like Paterson, N. J., or Lowell, Mass., than in a city of trade like Kansas City, Mo., or of State institutions, like Columbus, Ohio. The ratio of workingmen to the whole population has been variously estimated. Some think that only about one-third of the people in ordinary cities belong to that class. Others have estimated the proportion to be as great as four-fifths. It is my own impression that in the larger cities, at least, working-people rarely, if ever, compose less than one-half or more than three-fourths of the entire population. A fair average for American towns would perhaps be sixty per cent.*

It has always been difficult for well-to-do people of the upper and middle classes to sympathize with and

---

* See discussion of the subject in the work of Mr. John Rae, on *Contemporary Socialism,* pp. 348 and 349, London, 1884.

to understand the needs of their poorer neighbors. It
has been equally difficult for the workingmen to appreciate the position of those above them. Each class
is painfully conscious of the other's faults. Both are
blind to their own. The changes that modern times
have brought, do not lessen the difficulty. The development of mechanical invention has cheapened muscle-
work in comparison with brain-work. The income of
those engaged in the professions and in commercial
life has consequently increased much more rapidly than
that of the wage-workers. The contrast between the
condition of the two classes is every day becoming
greater and harder for the workingman to bear. Of
all the vast increase of wealth that the latter-day civilization has brought, he thinks that his share has been
pitifully small. He has a feeling that he has been used
unfairly, has been cheated out of hard earnings—a
vague impression that the upper ranks of society have
joined in some conspiracy against him and his toiling
brotherhood. The city's beautiful homes, splendid
with costly furniture ; the prancing horses and sparkling carriages ; the silks and seal-skins and the bright
and dainty dresses of rich children, seem to him to
have been filched from his own poor fireside and from
his shabby little ones. It is hard to approach a man
when he has a feeling that you and your class have
wronged him.

Civilization, in its onward march, has broadened the
breach between rich and poor in another way, and that
is by removing their homes from one another. The
price of bread may fall, the price of clothing may fall,
even the cost of meat may not increase so greatly ;
wages too may fall, but house-rent, never. Its course

is onward and upward. Mr. J. E. Thorold Rogers, a high authority, makes the statement that the value of land in England during the last four centuries has increased more than a thousand-fold on ground rents.* This rapid rise in rent has affected the poor and the well-to-do quite differently. The business man of moderate income finds the cost of the town house too great for him; but a few miles out from the centre of the city is another house, just as comfortable, and in some respects more so, which is within his means. So he lives outside the town and works within it, convenient trains carrying him to and fro every day. But it is not so with the workingman. When city rents become high he cannot follow his more fortunate neighbor to the suburbs. The expense of the daily railway ride would be a severe tax on his slender income, for one thing; experiments in England have also shown that the jar of the cars is peculiarly trying to those who are wearied by physical toil; but the main reason is that the length of his day's work makes it inconvenient to reside far away from his place of employment. In winter, a workingman who lives in the suburbs, must start for the town long before light in the morning and must take breakfast before that. He does not return to home and supper until long after dark at night. A hot dinner at some public house is a luxury that few can afford, and the cold dinner from the lunch-basket is hardly enough to sustain one through the long and toilsome hours from the hasty meal of early morning until the supper late at night. It is, moreover, undoubtedly true that the subtle

---

* Contemporary Socialism, *Contemporary Review*, Jan., 1885, p. 57.

attraction of the town's stirring life is peculiarly fascinating to working-people. Who does not know the difficulty of persuading domestic servants to take situations even a few miles out from the city? Many efforts have been made to induce the working-classes to exchange their crowded quarters in the towns for the more spacious suburbs ; but they have been usually attended with small success, the men preferring to put up with great inconvenience rather than move far away from their work. If, then, the rent of a house is more than one can afford, half a house must content him ; or if half a house is too dear, a quarter must suffice ; or if a quarter is still beyond his means, it must be a sixth or an eighth. Out of 114,759 families in Glasgow, 40,820 are living in one room each and 47,029 in two rooms each ; that is, seventy-eight families out of every hundred have only one or two rooms for their home. Less than one family in ten enjoys so many as four rooms.* There are, on the average, sixteen souls to every dwelling-house in New York City.† It is said that there are only about forty thousand old-fashioned "householders," that is, heads of families, who occupy a whole house by themselves in New York City. Most of the people live in "apartments."

Thus while the cities, spurred on by the spirit of the nineteenth century, grow and wax mightily, extending their borders on every side, the various elements of their society become with every year more widely separated from one another. The rich live beside the beautiful parks and along the broad and handsome

---

* *Census of Scotland*, 1881, vol. i., p. 313.
† *Tenth Census U. S.*, vol. i., p. 670.

avenues of "West End," or in some fashionable suburb amid velvet lawns and stately trees, from which they are at great pains to exclude omnibus and street-car lines, that none may come to live along with them save members of the select circle of carriage-keeping folk. Such of the middle class as live in town have their special quarters—long lines of street where the houses are smaller, rents lower, and the atmosphere less fashionable ; but the more distant suburbs, with a railway ride between them and the town, are getting to be the characteristic residences of the middle class. All about our chief cities, within distances of from five to fifteen miles, you will see sprightly little villages springing up, the houses new and neat, each in the centre of its patch of green, from which ranks of well-dressed men, armed with newspapers, go out at a comfortable hour in the morning to return at a comfortable hour at night   Such places have no troops of laborers marching forth at daybreak with their dinner-pails, no factory-girls, no drinking-saloons, no disorderly people about the streets by night, no paupers. All is peaceful and quiet and charming.   The schools are of the best ; the children may attend them safely, they need not mingle there with the rough and uncouth offspring of the poor.   The churches flourish greatly ; every pew is rented.

As for the workingmen and the poor, they are huddled together in ugly, dingy, ill-built dwellings about the docks and factories; they crowd some of the nearest suburbs, dreary and disagreeable to pass through, and they fill to overflowing the cramped tenements of certain unsightly and unsavory regions in some " North End " or "East End," where no one ever goes except landlords' agents, priests, and police. Between these poor districts and those where the richer class reside, there frequently lies the business portion of the city, a quarter overflowing with life and tumult by day, but silent and empty by night. The working-people are closely confined by their employment all day long and in the evening do not go far from home; so that the richer classes, especially in the larger cities, where the homes of the two are widely separated, see very little of them. It is "out of sight, out of mind." By the great majority of the upper class they are forgotten; their need and their just claims upon society are never thought of; their very existence is ignored until, in the shocking, lurid light of some violent strike or bloody riot, they are brought suddenly to notice. "Circum stances," says one of the most thoughtful workers among the masses of East London (a man who is also at home in the richest drawing-rooms of West End), "circumstances are daily giving to rich and poor the characteristics of two nations."

A keen critic of ourselves and our institutions remarks, that "society in America means all the honest, kindly-mannered, pleasant-voiced women, and all the good, brave, unassuming men, between the Atlantic and Pacific. Each of these has a free pass in every city and village, good for this generation only, and it depends on each to make use of this pass or not as it may suit his or her fancy."

We have reason for profound gratitude that so little of the spirit of caste has taken root upon our soil; that the best social circles are so accessible to all who deserve their privileges, without distinctions of rank or birth, and that even plutocracy does not reign supreme

5

within our borders. Yet to say that there are no social classes in the United States, especially in the cities of the United States, is to speak wide of the truth. We have, indeed, no titled nobility and little aristocracy. The distinction between upper and middle classes, if there be one at all, is vague and fanciful, and any barrier that may be raised between the two is thin, frail, and easy to break through. But with the working-class, the so-called "lowest class," it is quite otherwise. Here are found the same distinctions which characterize the cities of England, Scotland, and the continent of Europe. They spring from the same causes. They are aggravated by the same tendencies. They express themselves in the same class-prejudices. The workingmen are the first to recognize these distinctions, for their terms, "labor" and "capital," incorrectly as they use them, refer to divisions of society, the existence of which cannot be denied. A great and growing gulf lies between the working-class and those above them,—a gulf that is already as broad and deep —nay, in some respects, broader, deeper, and more difficult of passage in the cities of the United States than in those of Europe. Our own working-people are even more widely separated from the rest of society than those in England, France, and Germany, because the differences in occupation and wealth, which are becoming nearly as great here as there, are emphasized here as they are not there, by still greater differences in race, language, and religion.

This leads to a series of inquiries respecting the birth and nationality of our urban population.

"The world contains only two nations now," says a witty American, "those who speak English and those who don't." Mr. Mulhall shows that while the whole population of the world has doubled within a lifetime, the Anglo-Saxon race has quadrupled. The wonderful rapidity of this increase has been chiefly due to the growth of the United States, and the growth of the United States, as we all know, has been greatly accelerated by the flow of large streams from foreign sources into the Anglo-Saxon channel of the national life. We speak the language of Shakespeare as purely as it is spoken anywhere in the world; we claim the peerless literature of England as equally our own; we count ourselves the children and the heirs of that long succession of men and women who, by their mighty words and noble deeds, have made her history glorious. We hold to all that is best in her free institutions by a thousand bonds besides that of the common mother tongue; we find ourselves so closely knitted to the folk of old England that we can never think of them as foreigners. Yet we are not Englishmen or Anglo-Saxons, take us as a whole. The blood of many nations courses in hot and mingled currents through our veins. In Massachusetts the people are more than half of foreign birth or children of foreign-born parents. The same thing is true of New York and Rhode Island and several of the Western States. This mingling of peoples is the marked and special characteristic of the towns. Few of us realize how far from being Anglo-Saxon either in race, tradition, or religion are the cities of the United States. Those who come from foreign lands seem to be peculiarly attracted thither. They come as laborers, and the cities with their great industries are the labor-markets where they can best exchange for food that physical strength which is their only stock in trade. The proportion of foreign-born inhabitants is more than twice as great in the cities as in the whole country. We have two hundred and eighty-six considerable cities. The forty-four largest of these contain 34.2 per cent. of our total foreign population. These forty-four chief cities contain 38.7 per cent. of all the Germans in the land, 38.7 per cent. of the Bohemians, 45.26 per cent. of the Irish, 52.4 per cent. of the Poles, and sixty per cent. of the Italians.* If one could add to these amounts the number of foreign-born inhabitants in all the other two hundred and forty-two cities, we should doubtless find that fully three-fourths of our foreign-born citizens are city residents.

Because a man first saw the light in Europe it by no means follows that he is a foreigner. Thousands upon thousands of truest and most patriotic citizens have come hither from beyond the sea; neither does it follow because one is born on our soil that he is an American. More than one generation is required, under the ordinary conditions of urban life, to make the children of Irish and German peasants fit persons for citizenship in the great republic. Between the fathers who have come from the old country and the children born and bred in the new, there is always a marked difference; but frequently the change does not appear to be for the better. It is easy to learn the unfettered independence, the exemption from restraint that characterizes our institutions; but to know the law of liberty and to accept the responsibility which is wedded to freedom, is a more difficult matter. Thus it sometimes happens

---

* *Tenth Census of the United States*, vol. i., p. 470.

that the children of foreigners, being more used to the liberties, but quite as ignorant of the duties of citizenship, give greater perplexity to the preservers of order and purity than ever their fathers have done. A just and comprehensive view of the proportions of native and foreign blood, must therefore take into account not only the foreign-born, but also their children of the first generation. Regarding this matter, the census agents have brought to light as the result of a series of elaborate investigations extended to twenty-eight States, seven Territories, and the District of Columbia, certain facts from which the following general law may be gathered : that to every 100 persons of foreign birth, there belong, on the average, 115 children, parents and children together amounting to 215 ;* that is, in order to find out how many foreigners with their children reside in a given place, one must multiply the number of foreign-born as reported in the census tables, by 2.15. In this way we are made to realize to how great an extent American cities are European in population.†

---

* The parts examined with this object in view, contained 26,354,124 inhabitants, of whom 2,673,217 were found to be of foreign birth, while 5,758,811 were of foreign parentage. See *Tenth Census U. S.*, vol. i., p. 674.

† Thus it appears that out of one hundred persons in

New York	80	are foreign-born or children of foreign-born parents.
Philadelphia	51	" " " "
Brooklyn	67	" " " "
Chicago	87	" " " "
*Boston	63	" " " "
*St. Louis	78	" " " "
Baltimore	35	" " " "
Cincinnati	60	" " " "
*San Francisco	78	" " " "
*New Orleans	51	" " " "

The proportion of foreigners in a town depends largely upon its location and its prevailing industries. In the South, domestic service and all the simpler forms of labor are performed by the negroes. The proportion of foreigners in Southern cities is consequently small. New Orleans has, indeed, a large French element, which gives it fifty-one per cent. of foreigners with their children; but in Nashville, Tenn., they compose only eight per cent. of the population; in Charleston, S. C, only fourteen per cent., and in Richmond, Va., only eight per cent. In the national capital, where there are few manufactories and many colored people for domestic service, the proportion of foreigners is also small,—only twenty-five in a hundred. As a rule, manufacturing cities have more foreign-born than cities of trade. In Milwaukee and Detroit the foreign element comprises eighty-four persons out of one hundred. In Columbus, Ohio, and Kansas City, Missouri, the proportions are only thirty-six and forty-four out of a hundred. A few words as to the nationality of

Cleveland	80	are foreign-born or children of foreign-born parents.			
Pittsburg	61	"	"	"	"
Buffalo	71	"	"	"	"
*Washington	25	"	"	"	"
Newark	63	"	"	"	"
*Louisville	53	"	"	"	"
Jersey City	70	"	"	"	"
Detroit	84	"	"	"	"
*Milwaukee	84	"	"	"	"
*Providence	52	"	"	"	"

The census gives the actual figures for New York (vol. i., p. 675); those for the other cities were determined by the use of the above ratio, except in the cases marked by asterisks, where the census gives the ratio for the State in which they are situated, and that has accordingly been adopted.

our foreign population. It is composed of two great elements and a score and more of lesser ones. Twenty-nine and seven-tenths per cent. of our entire foreign population have come from various parts of the German Empire, and twenty-seven and four-tenths per cent. have come from Ireland.* Counting parents and children of the first generation, there were in 1880 four-fifths as many Irish in the United States as in all Ireland. New York is the first Irish city in the world, Philadelphia the third, Brooklyn the fifth, and Boston the sixth. Berlin and Hamburg are the only German cities that contain so many Germans as New York.

The Irish form the chief foreign element in the Eastern States. In Boston and most New England towns they outnumber all other foreigners put together. In New York, Brooklyn, Philadelphia, and all the other Eastern cities, except Baltimore, they are by far the largest class. They also head the list of foreigners in San Francisco, being more numerous by half than the Chinese. In the great cities of the interior the Irish are also strongly represented, and in none of the more important places are they rivaled in number by any other class of foreigners except the Germans.

Immigrants from the German Empire have never to any great extent made their home in New England. In New York, Brooklyn, Jersey City, and Philadelphia they are very numerous, and in Baltimore they even outnumber the Irish. In all the great cities of the in-

---

* It is probable that the Germans and Irish form a smaller proportion of the foreign population now than in 1880, when these figures were gathered, and that their relative numerical importance will continue to decrease, while that of Italians, Scandinavians, and others will grow.

terior, from Buffalo to Denver, the Germans lead, often outnumbering the Irish two to one ; and in such places as St. Louis, Cincinnati, Milwaukee, and Buffalo, composing, as the Irish do in so many Eastern towns, more than half the total foreign population.

The next most numerous element in our foreign population is that which comes from Canada and the British Provinces. This element is composed of three classes : there are, in the first place, considerable numbers of the regular English-speaking people of British America who are led by various motives to take up a residence in the United States. These are widely scattered throughout the country, but are most numerous in Boston, Buffalo, and Detroit. Then there has been, of late years, a large influx of French Canadians especially into the manufacturing towns of New England and the East, such as Lowell, Lawrence, and Fall River. In some of these places they are nearly as numerous as the Irish. A third class of immigrants from British America is composed of those who, having originally come to Canada from across the water, after a short residence there, have moved to the United States.

Our immigrants from England, Scotland, and Wales are not so fond of the city as the Germans and Irish. They are pretty evenly scattered over the whole of the North and West. Other nationalities are largely localized. New York City has the most of the Italians, although they are numerous in all the cities. The Swiss are found chiefly in New York, Chicago, and St. Louis; the Russians in New York and Chicago ; the Poles in New York, Chicago, Detroit, and Milwaukee ; the Swedes and Norwegians in Chicago, New York, Minneapolis, and St. Paul ; the Hollanders in Paterson, N. J.,

Chicago, and New York ; the Portuguese in Boston and
San Francisco ; the Danes in Chicago, New York, and
San Francisco ; the Bohemians in Chicago, New York,
Cleveland, and St. Louis ; the Spaniards in New York,
and the Chinamen in San Francisco and the towns of
the Pacific Slope.

While it is very common to find men of foreign blood
at the head of great mercantile enterprises and holding
other important positions in society, and while multitudes of such persons are engaged in the professions
and in trade, yet those thus employed form, on the
whole, an inconsiderable portion of our entire foreign
population. The great bulk of them with their children are engaged in the manual labor of the land.
They are the hewers of wood and drawers of water,
day-laborers, domestic servants, factory hands, and unskilled mechanics. Not every foreigner is a workingman ; but in the cities, at least, it may almost be said
that every workingman is a foreigner. The wage-
working class, especially that part of it engaged in
the simpler forms of labor, is almost entirely made up
of foreigners. How rare a thing it is, in these days,
to find a domestic servant who is of native parentage
or to meet a day-laborer who speaks without a brogue.
In the manufacturing and mechanical industries there
would, of course, be a much larger percentage of
Americans of native stock than among day-laborers.
Yet even among those thus engaged, in the fifty chief
cities, the census informs us that forty-one out of every
hundred were born in foreign lands, and it is probable
that quite as many more are children of foreign-born
parents.

We see, then, that of the two great classes which

divide the society of American cities between them, the smaller one, comprising those engaged in professions and trades, is principally composed of native Americans, while the larger class, the workingmen, are nearly all of foreign extraction.

Compare our position in this respect with that of the European cities and it will be seen that in none of them is the problem of the relation between the social classes complicated by such race differences as with us. London is one of the most cosmopolitan of the transatlantic cities. Strangers from all parts may hear their mother-tongue on its streets; yet out of every one hundred Londoners in 1880, sixty-three were natives of London, ninety-four of England and Wales, and ninety-eight of Great Britain and Ireland. The Emerald Isle furnished but two and one-tenth per cent. of London's population; and all foreign countries put together, only one and six-tenths per cent.* The same characteristics may be observed in Paris, Berlin, Vienna, and other foreign capitals.

But the race difference carries along with it another difference, which offers an even more serious obstacle to the safe solution of the social problem. The one great bond which alone can bind rich and poor together is that of religion. The one institution that can bridge the gulf between the classes is the church, and the only power that can hope to cope with cruel interference and grasping greed of the one party and the recklessness, drunkenness, and violence of the other, is that of the Gospel of Jesus Christ; but here the normal influences of religion are weakened and well-nigh destroyed by radical differences in faith and doctrine.

---

* *Census of England and Wales*, 1881, vol. iv., p. 59.

Ours is a Protestant land in name, institution, and tradition. Among Americans of native stock the proportion of Romanists is insignificant. It may, therefore, be said that the people engaged in the professional and mercantile occupations in cities are mostly Protestants.* The religion of the working-class, they being largely composed of foreigners and their children, as we have seen, may be determined by a glance at the religious condition of the countries from which they have come; for we may take it for granted that the children of the first generation, as a rule, continue to keep the faith of their fathers.

In the case of the Germans, our largest class of foreigners, we have made a somewhat careful investigation. Reckoning all who have come from Protestant parts as Protestants, and all from Catholic parts as Catholics, and supposing those who have come from parts where the population is divided between the two faiths to be divided in the same ratio, it appears that for every one hundred emigrants from the German Empire, thirty-eight are Roman Catholics and sixty-two Protestants.

As to the Irish, although one-fifth of the inhabitants of the Emerald Isle are said to be Protestants, those who have emigrated are nearly all Catholics.

The English, Scotch, and Welsh, on the other hand, are of the Protestant faith. So are the Scandinavians and a part of the Canadians; but the Italians, French Canadians, French, Mexicans, Poles, Austrians, Bohe-

---

* This is a very general statement. Jews and Roman Catholics are very numerous among the merchants, especially in some places, yet when compared with the whole number, they would form an inconsiderable proportion.

mians, and Belgians, for the most part, pay allegiance to the Pope. Adding together in one column the foreign born who, from their place of nativity, may be supposed to be Protestants, and in another, those who may be supposed to be Roman Catholics, the Catholics are found to be somewhat more numerous, the proportion being about that of 17 to 15. These figures give only an approximate idea of the proportionate strength of the two great branches of the Christian religion among our workingmen, yet they make it evident that at least one-half of them in ordinary American cities are Roman Catholics.

In the case of any particular town, the proportion would obviously vary with the prevailing element among the foreign-born population: the French and Irish cities being more strongly Catholic, the German and Scandinavian more strongly Protestant.

There is also a considerable difference between the Protestantism of the two social classes. English, Scotch, and Welsh find our American churches congenial, but it is otherwise with most of the Lutherans. Our creeds may not seriously disagree with theirs, but our ways and traditions are strange to them. Many have little sympathy with the stricter observance of the Lord's day and the inculcation of total abstinence as a Christian duty, with our more profound belief in the doctrine of regeneration and the religious methods and movements that result from it. We seem to them pietists and enthusiasts. Of all things, men are most conservative respecting their religious belief. It is hard for those who belong to religious bodies of one kind to influence those of another. The mother-tongue, long after it has vanished from commercial life and even from the family circle, still firmly holds its place in the pulpit. It is common to find among our Protestant Germans and Welsh that the families attend church where services are conducted in a language that the children cannot speak and can hardly understand. The common faith, therefore, forms a much weaker bond than one might wish between the Protestants of the working-class and those in other conditions of life.

And here again one cannot help contrasting our situation with that of the European cities. Most of them contain both Protestants and Romanists, although one element is usually strongly predominant; but in no case is there a division of religions corresponding with that of classes. The faith of the rich is ever the faith of the poor and the common bond between them. In the most splendid Roman churches you will see the titled lady in silk, the humble *contadina* with the basket by her side and the beggar, filthy and tattered, kneeling together on the marble floor. The richest and the most wretched are equally at home within the consecrated walls. From the mansions of West End, noblemen go down to the slums of East London and mingle freely with the people. Countesses conduct meetings for poor mothers and organize clubs for working-girls. In an English Christian home the servants are present at family prayers and attend the same church as their masters. But with us, especially in the cities, the church of the laborer is one, and the church of the well-to-do—or, as it is beginning to be called, " the capitalists' church " —is another.

I have thus endeavored to show that from one-half to three-fourths of the inhabitants of the cities are workingmen; that the natural separation between them and the rest of society has been broadened by the progress of mechanical invention which has cheapened the value of muscle-work in comparison with that of brain-work, and has thus increased the difference in wealth between the two classes, and by the rise of rents which has removed their dwellings from one another. And we have seen that the difficulty is greatly aggravated in the United States, because to the class-difference is added a race-difference, and to the race-difference, a difference in religious faith.

American cities, then, have two classes of people: the smaller, engaged in the professions and commercial life, is in comfortable circumstances, well-housed, well-clothed, and well-fed, is mainly of native stock and Protestant faith; the larger class toils with the hands, is less comfortable, worse housed, more coarsely and scantily clothed, and more poorly fed, is of foreign race and is largely Roman Catholic in religion.

CHAPTER III.

" Is our civilization perishable? " To this startling question, which a recent writer* answers in the affirmative, one's first impulse prompts the reply : "By no means. With Christian faith for the soul of it, the free school for its breastplate, and the printing-press for its weapon, the modern civilization can never perish." But careful attention to the perils of the times must modify the answer. If our civilization stands, this will not be because it is incapable of destruction, but because its sons and daughters, roused by its dangers, rally to its defence.

There can be no doubt that a state of society like the one in which we are living would be impossible except for the Christian religion. So vast and complex a structure as that of modern civilization could only stand on the solid foundation of public integrity. Unless the majority of the people were honest you could not have confidence and credit sufficient for the conduct of commercial transactions; unless a spirit of order and justice were abroad, property would not find secure protection and enterprise would be discouraged. Domestic purity is the corner-stone of civil liberty. Popular intelligence forms the chariot-wheels of progress. Thrift

---

Judge J. A. Jameson, *North American Review*, March, 1884.

and prosperity ever follow industry, economy, and temperance. The degree of advancement in any state depends chiefly upon the prevalence of such qualities as these among its citizens. But these qualities are distinctive marks of Christian character. They are the fruitage of the tree of faith, and never have been known as popular traits except in nations whose God is Jehovah.

Moreover, the degree of the nation's civilization depends upon the *purity* of its faith. The better the religion, the better will be the public integrity resulting from it; and the stronger its basis in public integrity, the higher will become the development and the more complex the organism of society. There is no need of showing that those countries in which degraded forms of Christianity prevail have lower standards of morals, and consequently lower degrees of civilization, than they enjoy who cherish a purer faith. Nor is there need of pointing out the truth that the evils which pervade our own land and sadly mar the beauty of its freedom, arise from the corruptness and incompleteness of our Christianity, our far-off following of our Master and our failure to accept His teachings and put His principles to practice. Many earnest men, indeed, are thinking that civilization in the most enlightened nations of the earth has reached a point where it falters, and can be urged no higher until men eschew the selfish plan of competition, which is now omnipotent in trade and industry, and substitute for it the essentially Christian principle of co-operation.

Now, if a community whose social system has been organized amid Christian influences and upon the Christian plan should at any time lose its religious faith, such loss would inevitably be followed by the slow decay of its morality, and the subsequent collapse of its civilization. The higher and more complex that civilization had become, the greater would be the ruin of its overthrow; for the body of Christian civilization cannot live without the soul. Let faith leave society and the lapse back toward barbarism will commence at once. Or if a purer and higher form of faith should give place to a lower and more corrupt form, such a civilization as had naturally grown up under the influence of the purer faith could not be sustained, but must certainly give place to civilization of a lower type.

Again, if from *any portion* of the society of modern times Christian life and power should be cut off throughout that portion the process of integration would speedily ensue. If from certain strata of the people the preserving strength of the "salt of the earth" be taken away, those strata, whether high or low, would forthwith commence sinking toward the normal plane of heathen living; and in their decay would bring distress, if not ruin, upon the whole of society. The portents of such perils as these are, as we believe, plainly to be seen in the present religious condition of American cities.

We have already observed that a gulf broad and deep divides the people of our towns into an upper and a lower class; and that by no means the smallest element in the difference between these two sections of society is a difference of religious belief. The pure high faith of our fathers, the faith that promoted at once free-thinking and right-thinking, power and purity, personal liberty and personal responsibility,—the faith on which the nation was founded, and through whose strength she has endured the shock of battles and stress of stormy times, — this faith has almost no place among the working-class. But the working-class holds a preponderance of power in the cities ; and the cities, already mighty, in their fearful growth, promise at no distant day to have a preponderance of power in the nation.

It will not be difficult to convince those who are acquainted with the life of our cities, that the Protestant churches, as a rule, have no following among the workingmen. Everybody knows it. Go into an ordinary church on Sunday morning, and you see lawyers, physicians, merchants, and business men with their families :—you see teachers, salesmen, and clerks, and a certain proportion of educated mechanics : but the workingman and his household are not there. It is doubtful if one in twenty of the average congregation in English-speaking, Protestant, city churches fairly belongs to this class; but granting the proportion to be so great as one in ten or one in five, even then you would have two-thirds of the people furnishing only one-tenth or one-fifth of the congregation. The recent experiment of an enterprising newspaper reporter in a certain American city which has the reputation of being the model Christian city of the world will not be forgotten. He donned the garb of a decent laborer, and presented himself for admission, at each in turn of the principal churches in the city. At some he was treated with positive rudeness, at others with cold politeness. Only one or two gave him a cordial, and even then a somewhat surprised welcome. The incident shows that in that city, at least, the appearance of a workingman at church on Sunday morning is not common.

The same thing is illustrated by the experience of those churches which have been so located that their former congregations have moved away from them, and in the course of the city's growth their neighborhood has been filled up by the working-classes How few have succeeded in holding their own, not merely in financial strength, but even in the size of the congregation, under such trying circumstances. Are not the down-town portions of the larger cities well supplied with old churches, that used on every Lord's day to be filled with worshippers? But now, deserted by their congregations, they stand idle and empty, or serve the purposes of trade, while the population about them grows ever denser. In a certain city whose case has been examined with some care, one denomination, and that the leading one, has but eight churches left in parts of the town more densely populated than ever, where it formerly had eighteen. Other denominations in the same city have not fared much better. Some marked exceptions are gladly noted, and there is a goodly number of God's people in every considerable town who are doing efficient work among the poor through missions, Sunday-schools, and a multitude of religious agencies; nevertheless, it must be allowed that the American Protestant Church, as a whole, has failed to win to itself the working-classes of the towns.

It is not claimed that religion consists in going to church, any more than eating consists in sitting down at a dinner-table; but as it may be presumed that whoever sits down at a table spread with food does so for the purpose of eating, so also we may presume that those who attend the services of God's house do so for the purpose of worshipping Him and hearing His word; and those who care for the word and the worship will not be more likely to neglect the sanctuary than a hungry man to neglect his dinner-table.

A word should be said regarding those Protestant churches which conduct their services in foreign languages. Some of these, notably the Welsh, and the German Methodists, Baptists, Presbyterians, Congregationalists, and others, are doing a work of great value; but they are still quite weak, and their influence correspondingly limited. The national churches of Germany, Norway, and Sweden have been transplanted to our soil to some extent, and are chiefly composed of workingmen. But, unhappily, they have not, in most cases, a strong, positive spiritual power over their adherents—a fact which none see more clearly and lament more bitterly than the more spiritual of their own members. There is said to be as much religious activity among the Christians of Berlin as in any of the larger German towns. Yet we find in that great city of one and one-third millions, only twenty-eight churches and thirteen chapels belonging to the established faith; and several of these are but thinly attended. Counting the establishments of the flourishing Young Men's Christian Association, the Catholic churches, the Jewish synagogues, the chapels of foreigners, and every place for religious gatherings of every sort, there are, in all, about sixty places of public worship in Berlin, or about one-tenth as many in proportion to the population as in New York. Nevertheless, eighty-five out of every hundred children born in Berlin are christened according to the rites of the established church, and the greater part of the people are confirmed at the proper age, and make it a point of duty to partake of the sacrament at stated periods. You accordingly find churches in Berlin whose membership numbers scores of thousands, while their seating capacity is sufficient for only a few hundred, and is even then rarely used to the full. The German churches, in being transplanted to our soil, have not changed their character materially, and are doing far less than might be desired in the way of establishing a living faith and an active righteousness among their followers. In many cases their grasp upon the people is very feeble. Not only do they reckon as members multitudes who do not attend*their services for years together, but there are thousands more who, leaving their religion behind them in the Fatherland, never take pains to connect themselves with the churches on this side of the water. It is a significant fact that while nearly all our Scandinavians, and the majority of our Germans, are nominally Lutherans, the Lutheran Church, in all its branches, together with the United Evangelical Church, and the United Brethren, had less than one million members in the United States at the time of the last census.*

In striking contrast with this is the condition of the Roman Catholic Church. It may be true that she holds her people with a looser grasp here than in Europe, and that she has altogether lost her influence over very considerable numbers of them; yet it must be acknowledged, on the other hand, that there have been surpris-

---

* In saying this we do not wish to speak unkindly of our German brethren, multitudes of whom are of distinguished piety, while their Christian scholarship has made all the world their debtors; nor would we ignore the powerful evangelical movement which the last few years have witnessed in the Fatherland, whose influence has been felt on this side of the water, and from which great things are to be hoped.

ingly few conversions from Romanism to Protestantism. Considering the fact that she has been compelled to push her system amid the full blaze of the light of modern times, in an atmosphere permeated with that spirit of freedom whose pure breath is her poison, the success of Rome in the United States appears amazing. There are, at the present time, about 7,000,000 of Roman Catholics (communicants) in the land.* In 1800 there were but one hundred thousand. It is less than one hundred years since the first bishop came to the United States. There were, in 1880, twelve archbishops, 55 bishops, 5,989 priests; there were 1,136 students in seminaries; there were 2,246 parochial schools, and 405,234 pupils.† The rate of increase for the Roman Catholic Church since 1850 has been more than twice as great as that of evangelical Protestant churches.‡

The Catholic Church is emphatically the working-man's church. She rears her great edifices in the midst of the densest populations, provides them with many seats and has the seats well filled. They are the places in which you never fail to find large congregations at the appointed times of public worship, the vast majority of whom are obviously workingmen and workingwomen. Here may be seen in great numbers, what many an earnest preacher of the reformed faith eagerly and vainly longs to behold in the pews before him, sons and daughters of toil clad in coarse garments with hard hands and plain, care-worn faces. The Cath-

---

* The official statistics for 1884 were, 6,628,176. This is the estimate of the *Independent*, May 19, 1887.

† *Sadlier's Cath. Directory*, 1880.

‡ For further treatment of this subject see *Our Country*, pp. 56 and 57.

olics make double the use of their houses of worship
that we do of ours. Three or four times on every Sunday great congregations pour forth from their doors,
whereas we are contented with but one or two meetings. Throughout the entire week their churches are
open, and one is rarely entered where a number of
people are not to be found kneeling in silent devotion.
Ours stand most of the time idle and empty, with
closely-locked doors. In this way a given number of
Catholic churches of a given size accommodate many
more people than Protestant churches of the same size
and number.

The religion of Rome is far better than none, and
we may well believe that many humble souls under the
leadings of the Spirit have found their way through
tangled meshes of falsehood with which she has cov-
ered it, down to the eternal truths on which her venerable faith is based. The influence of the Catholic
Church, on the whole, is doubtless conservative, and
will, probably, become more and more so. The Romanism of America is likely to be better than that of
Europe. Yet Romanism is not the religion we wish for
our fellow-citizens. It conceals the fatherhood of God
behind the motherhood of the Church, and the brotherhood of Christ behind the motherhood of the Virgin.
It degrades the atonement by making its benefits a
matter of barter; it leads to idolatry and image-wor-
ship; it snatches from the believer the great gift
bought with the blood of Christ, by thrusting in a
priest between him and his heavenly Father. It has
kept the people from the Word of God and compelled
them to accept forced and unscholarly interpretations
of it. It has lowered the tone of morality. It has

quenced free thought, stifled free speech, and threatens to throttle free government. It has limited the advancement of every country on which its hand has been laid. If the religion of Rome becomes ours, then a civilization like that of Italy will be ours too.

There is no more striking illustration of the alienation of the masses in the cities from the Protestant churches than the meagreness of their accommodations. If the laboring class should contribute its due proportion to the congregations, the churches, many of which are now half empty, would not begin to hold the people. In 1880 there was in the United States one evangelical church organization to every five hundred and sixteen of the population; in Boston, *counting churches of all kinds,* there was but one to every 1,600 of the population ; in Chicago, one to every 2,081; in New York, one to every 2,468; in St. Louis, one to every 2,800.* In New York below Fourteenth Street, where the people are principally laborers, there are only half as many Protestant places of worship in proportion to the number of people as above Fourteenth Street in the well-to-do parts.

The worst of it is, that instead of improving, the condition of things has been growing worse every year. While the prosperous classes are moving away to the suburbs and the laborers are being more densely massed together in the heart of the city, the church accommodations even if fully used are becoming more inadequate to the needs of the community. Look at the case of New York. Including religious organizations of all sorts, that city had in 1830 one place of

---

* It is true that the city churches are very much larger, but hardly four times as large.

worship for every 1,853 of its people; in 1840, one for 1,840; in 1850, one for 2,095; in 1860, one for 2,344; in 1870, one for 2,004; in 1880, one for 2,468. The religious history of Chicago is even more noteworthy in this respect. Chicago had in 1840 one church for every 747 of its population; in 1851 there was one for every 1,009; in 1862, one for 1,301; in 1870, one for 1,593; in 1880, one for 2,081; in 1885, one for 2,254. All the large cities have districts which are destitute of church accommodations, and have not seats in Sunday-school for more than one-tenth of their children.

The startling difference between the ratio of communicants in city and country furnishes another illustration of the fact that the workingmen who so largely people the cities are almost entirely cut off from the American Protestant churches. While in the country at large one person in five is a member of some evangelical church, in the city of New York it is only one in thirteen, and in Chicago one in nineteen. In the whole State of Ohio, cities included, more than one-fifth of the people belong to evangelical churches, but in Cincinnati only one in twenty-three. The alarming feature of the case, and that which we wish to emphasize, is that this small number of Christians in the community comes entirely from the upper class ; this one in twenty-three is almost never a workingman. The trouble is not merely that the cities have so little Christianity, but that the Christianity which they do have is confined to certain limited sections of society, leaving other sections, and those which comprise the great mass of the people, quite destitute of it, and practically heathen. Says Dr. A. J. Gordon, of Boston: "We talk about dangerous classes. The danger lies in the sepa-

ration of classes,—those who are the ' salt of the earth '
keeping by themselves instead of coming in contact
with that which tends to corruption. If the great mass
of Christians would come in heart-to-heart contact with
this so-called dangerous class much might be done to
change their character. But here is the failure. We
talk too much about family churches, and too little
about missionary churches."

One of the most serious evils consequent upon the
limitation of the church's operations to the well-to-do
classes is the reflex influence of such limitations upon
the church itself. The moment it ceases to be really
catholic, extending its blessings to all sorts and conditions of men, and becomes the organ of any class,
section or party, that moment it commences an unnat-
ural and unhealthful life. The rich need the poor no
less than the poor need the rich. That church which,
although situated in the midst of poverty and misfor-
tune, is for any reason restrained from stretching out
its hands to the needy, will itself suffer more seriously
because of such neglect than those from whom its suc-
cor is withheld. Avarice, self-indulgence, formalism,
arrogance, and hypocrisy are weeds of rank and ready
growth in a soil whose energy is not consumed in fruit-
bearing. Spiritual power decays ; the tremendous facts
of our faith appear dim and distant, and that which
should be a corps in the host of the living God, is degraded to the position of a musico-religious club, or a
mutual improvement society.

The reasons for the alienation of the working-classes
of the city from the faith of our fathers are not difficult
to find. The chief of them have already been sug-
gested. These people are foreigners, or the children of

foreign-born parents, almost to a man. The majority of them are of Roman Catholic training. The Catholics make it a point of great importance to give the Protestants a wide berth in all matters of religion. We Protestants seem to have consented to their plan. Whether we think that they have a religion good enough for their needs, or why it is we will not venture to say, but it is a fact that although our land is full of Romanists we make but few efforts to meet the peculiar difficulties that stand in the way of their conversion to the truth as it is in Christ. How many Christian families employ Catholic servants for years without paying any attention whatever to their spiritual welfare. Men are willing enough to supply their physical needs, but do nothing for the interest of their souls. We send missionaries abroad to Catholic Mexico, Spain, and Austria, but when a fellow-countryman is a Catholic, we accept it as a foregone conclusion that nothing can be done for him. They verily make greater efforts for our conversion than we do for theirs.

With some important exceptions those who come from foreign lands, both Catholics and Protestants, bring with them most crude and imperfect notions of religious truth. No Christian culture lies behind them. They have never breathed a Christian atmosphere. Ideas with which all the Americans, whether of pious parentage or not, have been familiar from childhood, are strange to them. For at least one generation their language shuts them out from the influence of our churches. The whole method of our services, adapted to the cultured, Christianized elements of society, is so far above them that it fails to secure their interest and attention. When one of them strays into a church, the chances are that he finds nothing there for him.

Much of the preservative power of the Christian religion comes from what may be called its indirect radiance. Christianity not only makes its followers virtuous, but it increases the virtue and intelligence of the whole community. When emigrants from the lowest classes of Ireland or Germany become so located in this country that they feel the influences of an intelligent, Christian community, they immediately respond to such influences, even though they still cling to the old faith, and their children helped forward by the public schools catch the spirit of our institutions and in due time become genuine patriots and valuable citizens. But unfortunately this is much less likely to be the case with those of foreign blood who live in large cities. Where from sixty to ninety people out of every hundred are of foreign parentage, and the residences of the natives are so separated from those of the foreigners that contact between them is neither close nor frequent, it is a slow process raising the ignorant, degraded peasants of Europe to a place of fitness for citizenship in our democratic republic.

One of the most hopeful features of the times is the appreciation of education and the desire to give their children a schooling which is manifest among our workingmen. But the public schools do not give a moral and religious training of great value. Moreover, extreme poverty and the needs of growing families make it necessary for most working-people to take their children from school and put them to work as soon as they are old enough to contribute to the family budget. The "three R's," with a smattering of geography, is all that the schools usually give them. This is a good deal better than nothing, however, and most of them at odd times manage to gather a considerable fund of information from books and newspapers. We are confident that our workingmen do much more reading than those of the old world, and are correspondingly more intelligent; but on the other hand, there is reason for fearing that much of their reading is not particularly profitable. The circulation of sensational "family" story papers and second-rate sporting papers in this country is prodigious, and is rapidly increasing. Thousands of the well-known advertisement copies commencing and not finishing the trash stories of such publications are given away every week in all the towns. They are handed out in unlimited quantities to shop-girls and laborers as they return from their work, most frequently on Saturday night, and they are not usually refused or thrown away, but are carefully folded and placed in the lunch-basket; a thing the like of which is to be seen in no foreign city. Such reading answers about as well for mental food as rankly-flavored confections would for honest bread. And there is little doubt that much of the reading done in the workingman's home is of this class.

Theoretically, their participation as sovereign voters in our free Christian government ought to do much for the development of intelligence and self-reliance among the workingmen. And so it would were our Government conducted on the original plan of the New England country town, where every item of administration is freely discussed in the presence of all the voters at the annual town meeting; but no one is wild enough to claim that such contact with average ward politicians as constitutes the political education of the ordinary city laborer can contribute greatly either to his mental or moral advancement.

The other great reason for the feeble influence of Protestant Christianity over the working-class springs from the so-called conflict between labor and capital. As we have already seen, the wealth of all Christendom, and that of the United States in particular, has enormously increased during the past twenty-five years. The census of 1880 estimated the wealth of the nation at $43,642,000,000, which makes us the richest nation in the world. If our wealth had been equally distributed in 1860, each person's share would have been $514; in 1870 it would have been $624; in 1880 it would have been $ 14, for every man, woman, and child in the land. During those twenty years the population increased 9 per cent., the wealth more than 151 per cent. A very small share of this increase has gone to the workingman. In certain important respects he is poorer to-day than twenty-five years ago. Wages are indeed higher in comparison with the cost of living, and many comforts and luxuries have been so cheapened as to come within his reach. Science and invention have also made certain valuable additions to his home; but his progress has been slow at best, and his neighbor, the business man, has far outstripped him in the race for wealth.

Wealth and poverty are, after all, only relative terms. As Mr. Emerson has said : "The poor are only those who feel poor, and poverty consists in feeling poor." In this sense of the word the American workingman was never before so poor as to-day. If his income has increased, so have his wants, and far more rapidly. What boots it to tell a man whose coat is worn and shabby, and whose shoes are breaking through, that people of his class a hundred years ago wore coarser clothes and had never a shoe to the foot? Is that a reason why he should go tattered and barefooted while multitudes about him revel in luxury? Because a man's father in Ireland or Germany never knew the taste of meat, and lived on black bread and potatoes, does it follow that he ought to suffer the like privations? By no means is the workingman ignorant of the enormous increase of these latter days. Instead of under-estimating them, he holds exaggerated notions of the riches of the rich, while he fails to note such improvements as time has brought in his own condition. Recent labor statistics show that the workingman is better off now than twenty years ago. But the men themselves affirm, on the contrary, that things are growing worse from year to year,—the wages lower, the work harder and more uncertain, and the prospect of promotion more and more hopeless.*

Now the workingmen, as a class, are coming to believe that the bulk of the wealth of modern times belongs to them, all wealth being, as is claimed, the fruit of toil. It has sprung from the brawn of their arm and the sweat of their brow. Capital has but furnished tools, they have done the work and won the rewards; to them, therefore, those rewards belong. But instead of receiving what is their own, they have been cheated out of nine-tenths of it by grasping capitalists, who are protected in their plundering by unjust laws and a tyrannical social system. There is a bitterness about the discontent of these men They feel that they are being robbed every day and cannot help it. The de-

---

* The writer has conversed on this subject with a number of workingmen engaged in various occupations both here and in England, and finds but one opinion among them.

mand for work is so great that however hard the job and low the wages, a dozen men stand ready to take a place as soon as it is left vacant.

A street-car driver in a certain American city gave the following account of his work, which was afterward confirmed: He is occupied seventeen hours a day seven days in a week. He has, out of this, ten minutes for dinner, and nine for supper. He can get but five or six hours for sleep. All the work connected with that car he does himself. Even the hostler's pay comes out of his wages. The car, at a reasonable estimate, earns $108 50 each week, after deducting the cost of feeding the horses that draw it, of which sum $97.50 goes to the company, and $11 to him; but he finds that from sheer want of sleep he must usually " lay off " one day in the week; $1.57 is, therefore, taken to pay for a substitute. The care of the horses costs him seventy cents more. Therefore, out of the entire receipts of the establishment, he who bears the burden, braving the winter's bitter breath, and the fiercest heat of summer; the wind, the storm, and the weather, every day from dawn until midnight—this man receives but $8.73 while capital's share is $97.50. This poor driver thinks that he is cheated; that the company is robbing him, in a systematic and legalized fashion, every day. They have the advantage over him; he cannot help himself; he must work on their terms or starve; but he hates them, grinds his teeth at them, and haply would not count it stealing if he could get some of their dimes into his own pocket.*

---

* This case is introduced to show that there is never a lack of men who are willing to take the most trying and miserably-paid-for kinds of work. The writer is glad to believe that few street railway com-

The ill-will of the laborer toward the capitalist is greatly increased by periods of business depression. When so many mills are closed, and factories stand idle, it is hard for the worker to understand that his employers are no more to be blamed for such occasions than he himself; and that employers frequently, if not usually, do the very best they can for their hands, both in the matter of high wages and that of regular work. Most wage-workers live from hand to mouth. They must necessarily do so if, as economists say, the price of labor is measured by the lowest cost of living. In Massachusetts, the average expense of the laborer's household, in 1884, was greater by $196 than the earnings of the head of the family. This extra expenditure had to come from the earnings of the wife and children. No wonder only one in a hundred of them owned his own house! When the mill stops, the supply of daily bread is cut off. The grocer gives credit for a while; after that, if there is still no work to be had, pauperism. Work is hard to get at such times. Hard enough at any time. You will find idle laborers gathered in drinking-saloons and on street corners always talking on one inexhaustible theme—the oppression of labor by capital.

In some cases the closing of mills has been justly and extremely provoking to employés. Those engaged in a certain line of manufacture, finding that more is being produced than can profitably be sold, meet together and form a pool,—that is, an agreement is made in accordance with which some of the mills are closed, and

---

panies abuse their men in this fashion. In Boston, they are employed from twelve to twelve and one-half hours a day, out of which an hour is allowed for meals.

7

suffered to stand idle until the "over-production" of such goods is checked and their price raised, and the owners of the idle mills are meanwhile paid out of the common purse for the losses incurred in closing them. Thus the owner's income continues as regularly as ever, although the factory doors are closed and its chimneys smokeless. But the working-people who were wont to depend on that mill for support—no one pays them for the silence of its looms and spindles. They must consume the little laid up for old age; they must commence the weary search for work elsewhere, and perhaps be reduced to destitution before they find it.

The reader need not be reminded of the extent to which trades-unions and labor-unions and the strikes and disorders that have been promoted by them have broadened the breach between the workingmen and their employers. Whether they have done anything to help the cause of labor may be doubtful. This much, however, is certain, that they have done very much to rouse and spread abroad among the working people a hatred for those classes whom they have been taught to call "oppressors."

Listen to the workingman himself. We quote from the *Iron Moulder's Journal* for January and February, 1885. It is not a socialist's paper, but a sober, conservative labor organ ; neither are these articles selected carefully, but are taken from such numbers as were at hand, and fairly represent the spirit in which these matters are usually discussed in such circles :

"One hundred workers, of as many occupations, will produce, working as they now work, treble the amount of all the necessities and comforts that one family will consume. How in God's name is it that they cannot get enough to eat and wear? What is it, and who is it that takes it all from them and grudgingly doles back to them just sufficient to keep body and soul together for not the allotted life of man, but for the time necessary to work and starve them into the grave?"

Again we read: "The working-classes, without distinction of trades, have never, in the history of this country, suffered as they are now suffering. The year opens with labor, as a rule, almost completely at the mercy of capital, and capital gloating over its power to inflict the most cruel pangs upon labor, and exercising that power with a venom which will work inevitable retribution."

These people are saturated with hatred for the whole class whom they term "the capitalists," a hatred that is often unreasoning and unreasonable, that is usually sweeping and intense.

Now, city churches of the Protestant order are usually attended and sustained by persons of means and intelligence. It makes a man prosperous to be a Christian. The Protestant city churches are, therefore, to the laborer, the churches of the capitalist. He will have nothing to do with them. Their cushions and carpets, their polished pews, stained windows, and pealing organs, as well as the rich garments of their prosperous congregations, were purchased, as he thinks, with money wrested from his toil-worn fingers. What wonder that the invitations of the church ring in his ears like tones of hollow mockery, from which he turns away with a bitter heart! This, after all, is the chief of the reasons why workingmen so rarely enter the door of a Protestant city church. They identify the churches with the capitalists, and the capitalists they count their enemies.

We have thus endeavored to show that the working-men of American cities are almost wholly shut out from the direct, and largely from the indirect influences of Protestant Christianity, by their foreign birth, training, and religious traditions, and also by the peculiar nature of the relations between the laborer and the capitalist. If, now, the propositions with which the chapter opened are true; namely—that the body of Christian society cannot exist without the soul, and that so soon as Christian influence is withdrawn from even a portion of society, that portion must forthwith lapse toward barbarism at the peril of the whole—if these are true, we should expect to see tokens of such a catastrophe in the American cities to-day, and such tokens are not lacking.

Consider, for example, the matter of municipal government. There is no need of enlarging upon the well-known fact that the governments of most of our important cities have for a long time been more or less rotten, and in some cases little more than gigantic systems of fraud. It has been frequently observed that if it were not for the control of State legislation life and property would hardly be safe within them. And now that State legislatures are more and more coming under the control of the gangs from the cities it is time that sober men were awakening to the seriousness of the situation. But let us ask, what is the significance of such a state of things? What does it mean when New York aldermen are convicted of receiving bribes by the wholesale ; when Chicago mayors laugh at the laws of the land and snap their fingers in the face of those who urge their execution; when Cincinnati juries refuse to bring verdicts against criminals of undoubted

guilt? Does it not mean that the people by whose suf-
frages such officials have obtained their positions are
either too ignorant or too immoral for self-govern-
ment?

Or consider, again, the drunkenness of the cities.
The fearful statistics of the vice need no repetition.
But it should not be forgotten that, unlike the churches,
the drinking-saloons find the majority of their patrons
among the workingmen. A machine moulder recently
said to the writer that he did not know a person in his
trade who is not a drinking man. Drinking-saloons
are both causes and effects of a city's degradation.
They are effects; they come where poverty makes the
home dingy, squalid, and unattractive. Day and night
their doors are open, offering to the weary laborer
retreats that, with their polished brass and stained
glass, their light and warmth and cheery company, are
immeasurably more attractive than his home. Apart
from the drinking, the drinking-places have a strong
fascination for their patrons; but the drink too is made
the more enticing by the misery of the drinker. Exhausted by long hours of monotonous labor, or by a
still more trying search for labor when "out of a job,"
the man has an irresistible craving for some stimulus
which will lighten his heart and banish his sorrows for
an hour. The relief is close at hand ; it is cheap and
easy to take. That "at last it biteth like a serpent and
stingeth like an adder," no one knows better than they
who are most familiar with the ruin of it. But those
that have the least are the most reckless. For the sake
of relieving present discomfort they are willing to run
the risk of future misery. You find the saloons thickest in the poorest quarters.

Drinking-places are also *causes* of an inestimable deal
of ruin. Besides actual drunkenness and the ghastly
train of disease and crime that follows it, there is a
moral poison about the grog-shops whose deadly power,
though less frequently recognized, is scarcely less per-
nicious. A hellish atmosphere pervades these places.
They are full of profanity, indecency, and infidelity,
the headquarters of political corruption and the hot-
beds of crime. It would be very unjust to put them
all on a level. Some are certainly much more respectable than others ; but none of them are too good, and
the tendency of all is downward. These are the places
where many of the workingmen most frequently meet
and spend the greater part of their leisure. In halls
connected with them labor unions and even building
societies usually hold their sessions.

According to the census of 1880 the city of Boston
had one saloon for every 329 persons ; Cleveland, one
for 192; New York, one for 179; Chicago, one for 171;
and Cincinnati, one for 124, or one for every twenty-five
families. This calculation does not include groceries or
drug-stores where liquor is sold. The amount of drinking has been increasing from year to year. Do not
these facts betoken a serious decline from the high
plane of Christian civilization?

Other evidence in the same direction appears in the
increase of crime that the past thirty years have witnessed. In 1850 Massachusetts had one prisoner to
804 of the population. In 1880 she had one to 487.
The criminal population in proportion to the whole
population had nearly doubled in thirty years. The
report of the prison commissioners for Massachusetts
for 1884, shows that the entire number of arrests for

the year ending September 30, 1883, was 65,000, or one arrest for every twenty-nine of the population. Who these offenders were becomes evident when you read that Suffolk County, the county of Boston, had in proportion to its population more than twice the number of prisoners of any other county, and five or six times as many as those counties that do not include large towns.

The census makes an even worse showing than this for the whole country. Between 1870 and 1880, the population of the United States increased 30 per cent. Meantime crime in the United States increased 83.32. The superintendent of the police reports that in Chicago, in the year 1883, there were 37,187 arrests in that city, or one for every sixteen of the population. Of these, 159 were for murder, manslaughter, and intent to kill. The same sad story comes from every great city of the land, and one of its saddest features is the increase of what may be called seed crimes—those of the women and boys. Have we not here, too, ominous indications that the foundations of Christian civilization are rotting away beneath us?

The increase of poverty and pauperism is another token of the same thing. This was one of the heaviest chains that dragged old Rome down to the dust. The public statement was recently made that from one in twelve to one in fifteen of the inhabitants of Ohio received charitable aid in the course of a single winter.

The Massachusetts State Board of Charities reports that in 1855 16 persons out of every 1,000 received aid; in 1860 the number was 28 ; in 1865, 36 ; in 1870, 45 ; in 1875, 121 ; in 1880 the number was not reported, but the expenditure was greater by 6 per cent. than in 1875.

In a paper read before the Congregational Club of New York City, Mrs. Josephine Shaw Lowell showed from the records of the City Charity Organization Society that during three years two hundred and twenty thousand nine hundred and sixty-seven different persons, or about one-fifth of the entire population of that city, had asked for outside charity in one form or another.

"The bitter cry of outcast London," which has reached us across the sea, telling of hundreds of thousands in that most Christian of cities living in such filth, misery, ignorance, nameless vice, and unspeakable degradation that all heathendom has not the like of it, shows the condition toward which our own poor folks are daily sinking.

Another token of the same thing is seen in the desecration of the Christian Sabbath. Can we have Christian civilization without a Sabbath day? Granting that the Puritanic Sabbath is not adapted to the needs of our time, no one will deny that we need some sort of a Sabbath day,—a day, too, which in all essential elements shall not be one whit inferior to that which our fathers handed down to us. Where is the city in which the Sabbath day is not losing ground? To the mass of the workingmen Sunday is no more than a holiday. The conception of it that they have brought with them from Europe has not been improved. It is a day for labor meetings, for excursions, for saloons, beer-gardens, base-ball games, and carousals.

As a final token of the threatening dissolution of the fabric of Christian society, notice the nature of the new gospel for workingmen which many of the socialists are preaching. This is not the place for the dis-

cussion of socialism. We have no time to speak here
of its wide and rapid spread in our own country and
all over Europe, nor to consider how much of what is
true and valuable may be mixed up with its teachings ;
nor can we notice the extent to which it has influenced
the thinking of multitudes who have not accepted its
doctrines as a whole—an influence clearly seen in recent
labor troubles, in the late elections, in the formation of
the Anti-Poverty Society, etc. But the thing to be observed is the tendency of the doctrines that are at
present advocated by its leaders. The International
Workingmen's Association, which is the principal social-
istic society in this country and the world, makes it its
direct purpose to promote the very thing which, as we
have tried to show, is now threatening us, namely: the
overthrow of the present system of society. These
anarchists have most vague and varied notions of what
should take the place of that which they wish to destroy. Whenever they attempt to tell how the new
society should be organized, they become involved in
hopeless confusion. The one plan upon which they all
agree is that of destruction. Many of the leaders go
so far as to advocate the abolition with private property
of religion, the State, the Church, and even the family.
Give such men their way, not that they are likely to
get it, and they would dash the proud temple of civilization with a single blow to the ground, and leave the
world in as dense a darkness of barbarism as ever en-
veloped our fathers of the Northland. It is hoped that
these will not be regarded as the extravagant words of
an alarmist. So surely as God is faithful, that Gospel
which Jesus Christ brought to the poor must reach the
poor, or else they, perishing in their blindness, will in-

volve all Christendom in common ruin. Are not these things already rolling in upon us like a mighty storm-cloud,—this increasing drunkenness and crime, this Sabbath desecration, this pauperism, this lawlessness and strife between rich and poor, this worse than heathen poverty and degradation? Do you answer, "Oh, well, but the cities have always been full of drunkenness, poverty, and disorder; they are the fever-sores of the land"? True: but do not forget that while the "fever-sores" grow redder and more angry, they are growing larger every day. It was a comparatively small thing that the cities were vicious when they contained one-thirtieth of the people, but now they contain nearly one-fourth; soon it will be one-third, one-half; such fever-sores must not be ignored.

That soil where weeds grow rankest is ever a fertile soil, capable also of yielding rich harvests of grain. If the towns of modern times furnish extraordinary facilities for the deadly work of the destroyer, at the same time they give no less advantage to the armies of salvation; they afford unrivalled fields for the triumphs of the Redeemer. God has rarely given His servants greater opportunities for doing good, and bringing forth much fruit unto His praise, than one can find in the troubled hearts of the great cities to-day: for the "sword of the Spirit" is never so mighty as when wielded amid the multitudes.

CHAPTER IV.

THE whole world centres in London: thither all paths lead, and all lines of life converge. As it is the focus of the earth's population, the headquarters of polite society and political power, the emporium of trade and a chief seat of art, science, and literature—even so, London stands at the very thickest point of the great world-battle between good and evil. There the strongest concentration of Christian power is pitted against the most formidable foes to the faith and the life that are in Christ. There the most urgent problems of the age are pressing hardest, and there, as in no other place, are time and treasure devoted to their solution. A study of the methods of work adopted by the churches of the world's metropolis should, therefore, be helpful to those whom the same service employs in other parts of the field.

Religious work in London deals with a society which differs from that of our own cities widely and in many respects. The social gamut is broader than here, and the class distinctions more marked and more generally accepted. It is the city at once of the greatest wealth and the greatest poverty; in few places is living so costly, yet millions there have but a few shillings a week on which to live. We of America know of no such

wide contrast—almost like that between men and beasts
— as the one which separates the aristocratic top of
English society, with its exquisite culture, vast wealth,
and sumptuous luxury, from the miserable bottom.
The city of the Thames appears like some strange
woman whose haughty head flashes with diamonds,
and whose upper garments are of silks and gems, while
her worn and faded skirts drag tattered fringes through
the mire and filth of squalid streets.

The fierceness of the struggle for existence is not yet
so keenly felt in the new world. Want and over-crowd-
ing have thus far forced comparatively few of our poorest families to the degradation of the one-room life that
so largely prevails in the lowest parts of London.
There is much more alms-giving to be done there than
here. They have more of the hungry, naked, and home-
less needing their ministry; more need of asylums,
hospitals, refuges, and houses of mercy. The dullness,
drudgery, and hardships of their lives have stamped
themselves in woful lines upon the sallow faces of the
poor. During large portions of the year the murky
atmosphere admits but little sunshine, and the lot of
the working-people is correspondingly sunless and
leaden-hued; the church is, therefore, loudly called
upon to pour whatever of brightness she is able into
their cheerless homes and over their joyless lives.

The vastness of the need of London is paralyzing to
benevolence; the effort to relieve it seems hopeless. It
is like trying to fill a bottomless pit, or casting handfuls
of earth into the sea. The ocean of human misery
swallows up everything it receives, and shows no
change. Pauperism and the pauper-spirit greatly en-
hance the difficulty of Christian work. There are mul-

titudes of poor wretches with whom religion is only a means of getting bread and butter. Nothing is more difficult than to win such people to Christian manliness.

On the other hand, they do not share some of our greatest difficulties. As we have already seen, the foreign population is small in comparison with our own, and the Roman Catholic Church has not a strong foothold, and almost none among the lower classes of English blood.*

Other elements of the religious problem, and those the most important, our cities possess in common with those of Great Britain. In both countries the towns are growing with great rapidity, making the utmost diligence necessary that the appointments of religion keep pace with the increasing population. In both this growth is broadening the gulf between rich and poor, so that those parts which have the greatest need of churches are least able to build and sustain them. In both there are the same evil influences of factory life and bondage to machinery. Both have the same industrial questions; the same struggle and jealousy between labor and capital, and the same alienation of the working-people from the church, on the ground that it is an aristocratic institution conducted in the interest of the wealthy classes, and bent upon keeping them in subjection to the capitalists; and in both there is the same determination on the part of thousands of God's people to establish juster and more intimate relations between rich and poor, and to distribute the benefits

---

* There are forty-seven Roman Catholic churches in London, against about sixteen hundred Protestant churches; but the former are, on the average, of greater size.

of Christian civilization more uniformly throughout society.

Seeing that there are not less than sixteen hundred Protestant churches in London, and so many charitable institutions that an account of them, in which each is briefly described, fills a volume of a thousand pages,* any complete and careful description of the religious and benevolent work in that city is, of course, out of the question here. We shall confine ourselves to a mere outline of general methods pursued by our English brethren in church work, especially that intended for the benefit of working-people, and shall illustrate this by more extended notice of two or three such movements as have come under our own observation.

We naturally begin with the Established Church. This body had in the metropolis, at last accounts, besides St. Paul's Cathedral and Westminster Abbey, nine hundred and twenty churches, and a large number of mission halls and schools.

The cathedral and the abbey differ from the churches in being unconnected with a parish, and in being controlled by a Dean and Chapter of Canons instead of a single clergyman, as well as in their vaster size. It used to be the case that these stately piles had very little to do with the practical religious work of the church, and the ecclesiastical offices connected with them "were considered little less than dignified sinecures"; but the church of to-day aims to make them centres of spiritual life and power.† The chief office

---

* *Charities Register and Digest*, with an introduction by C. S. Loch, Secretary to the Counsel of the Charity Organization Society, London, 1884.

† See Work of the Church of England during the Present Century, by Rev. Canon Gregory. *National Review*, vol. ii.

which they perform is that of supplying regular and very frequent religious services with the most eloquent of preachers and sweetest-voiced choirs.

In St. Paul's there are six regular services on every day in the week except Sunday. One of these is a celebration of the holy communion, and two are choral services held in the body of the cathedral. The others are held in chapels and the crypt. On Sundays there are only four regular services with two celebrations of the holy communion. These services are varied on holy-days by additional sermons and special music. During Lent, for example, there are nine additional sermons weekly. The services in Westminster Abbey are somewhat less frequent, and the early morning celebration of the communion occurs only on Sundays and holy-days. It is the custom during Lent and the Advent to perform some great musical work in connection with the cathedral services, such as Bach's *Passion Music*, Handel's *Messiah*, or Spohr's *Last Judgment*. This custom is also followed in some of the parish churches. The singing in the cathedrals and larger parish churches is led by trained choirs of boys whose clear voices have a peculiar quality of exquisite, passionless sweetness scarcely human and more like flute-notes, or the songs one would expect from the cherubs that hover in the mist of glory about Raphael's madonnas. The more difficult portions of the music are, of course, rendered by the choir alone, but the congregations heartily join in most of the singing. We have no more important lesson to learn from our English cousins than that of congregational singing.

Besides the regular and frequent services already mentioned, the cathedrals are used for great occasional gatherings such as Sunday-school festivals and anniversaries of religious societies.

The parish churches seldom hold less than three regular services on Sunday, one of which is usually designed for children, and nearly all of them have regular and frequent week-day services. Canon Gregory reports that of the nine hundred and twenty churches of the Establishment in London, two hundred and eighty-six have a daily service, five hundred and twenty-five celebrate the holy communion every week, and forty-seven every day, while only one hundred and twenty-two have no week-day services.

Various means are used, apart from the regular services, to quicken and foster spiritual life among the churches. For the clergy there are *quiet days*, or *retreats*, as they are called. These are devotional meetings for spiritual refreshment extended through one or two days and conducted by men whom age and experience, as well as natural endowment, have given peculiar fitness for the service.

Parochial missions, like that held in the winter of 1885-6 in Trinity Church, New York, are becoming a marked feature in the life of the Church of England. In purpose and methods they closely resemble our own revival-meeting and protracted services. They aim "to rouse the careless and indifferent and to excite increased earnestness and devotion on the part of those who make a profession of religion." Several neighboring churches usually unite in such a mission and special preparation is made for months before its services begin. Those most interested meet daily to pray for its success; the neighborhood is thoroughly canvassed, invitations to the extra meetings are widely scattered, the factories are visited and brief addresses given to the employés at the noon hour, and the meetings within the church are frequently preceded by brief open-air services without.

Bible Classes and *Communicants' Classes* are conducted by the majority of the churches, and most of them have annual confirmations, for which catechumens are prepared by a regular course of instruction lasting several weeks or even months.

Societies or *Guilds* for the promotion of spiritual life are frequent both in the congregations of the Established Church and among nonconformists. One of these, which may be taken as an example, states that its object is " to promote the glory of God by individual holiness and some useful service undertaken in His name." " Its members are bound together by the keeping of a simple, practical rule of life, by daily use of the guild prayer and by the meeting together twice every month, once at early celebration of the holy communion, and once for a devotional meeting." Many of the guilds have printed cards specifying a series of daily Bible-readings which all the members agree to follow. There are also guilds for boys, whose members agree to say their prayers kneeling every night and morning, to attend church at least once every Sunday, and when confirmed to "communicate" once a month. It is the practice to have "guardians" appointed over sections of the boys' guilds, whose office it is to act as friends to the lads placed under their care. These men find large opportunities for useful service as counsellors in their young wards' affairs, both those of business and of pleasure; they attend the regular meetings of the guild, look up absentees, visit the sick

8

and assist those who are in trouble. Similar guilds have been formed for women and girls.

Most of the larger churches employ more than one clergyman, and some of them as many as three or four. Besides these, there are usually several missionaries, Bible-women, deaconesses, and trained nurses working in the parish under the superintendence of the rector.

A strong movement has been made during the past few years in the direction of extending ecclesiastical work to the laity. London has an organization entitled *The Lay-Helpers' Association*, with an enrolled membership of above five thousand. These "lay helpers," or "lay readers," are employed as teachers of Bible-classes, superintendents of Sunday-schools, to hold services and preach in halls and unconsecrated buildings, and to engage in mission work of every sort. Many of the churches have also organized *bands of visitors*, among whom the poorer portion of their parishes is so distributed that every family is allotted to some one of them. Visitors of this kind are often willing to accept fields of labor in other parishes than that of their own residence and in poor and distant portions of the town.

One of the most important agencies employed both by the Church of England people and the Nonconformists in their work among the poor—the one which is usually first to take definite shape in commencing a mission of any kind—is a weekly gathering of poor women, called *the mothers' meeting*. It is conducted by some lady of superior ability, often assisted by other ladies and by a "Bible-woman." The latter belongs to the humbler class of society, and is, therefore, a more useful and welcome visitor to the homes of the poor

than those of higher rank. In their meetings the poor
women are taught to make and mend garments properly; they have practical talks on cooking and nursing,
and other domestic matters; suitable selections from
books and periodicals are read to them; music is employed to win and interest them, and religious instruction is not neglected. *Clothing-clubs* are nearly always
connected with the mothers' meetings; that is, arrangements by which flannel, prints, and garments
may be bought in small quantities at wholesale prices.
Sometimes coal and grocery clubs, conducted on the
same principle, as well as penny banks, are added.
Members are encouraged to deposit a few pence each
week until they have accumulated enough to pay for
some coveted garment or article of furniture. Poor
mothers are very fond of these meetings, which often
form a single bright spot in lives that are otherwise
dark and dreary enough. Some of them are very large.
The writer visited one which had about nine hundred
members, and was obliged to hold its meetings in two
sections. They are extremely useful in opening the
hearts and homes of the poor to religious influences,
and afford opportunities for certain sorts of instruction
and help that the regular services of the Church could
never supply.

Another agency employed by the Church of England
among the poor is *The Girls' Friendly Society* * This is
one of the most useful and important branches of
benevolent work in England, and aims to meet the needs
of a class whose claims on the help and sympathy of
the well-disposed are not surpassed by those of any

---

* See account of this society by the Countess of Shrewsbury, entitled Prevention. *Nineteenth Century*, Dec., 1885.

other. The movement was commenced about ten years ago, under the auspices of the late Archbishop of Canterbury and Mrs. Tait. It enjoys the patronage of Her Majesty the Queen, the Princess of Wales, and other members of the royal family, as well as the Archbishops of York and Canterbury. Although of national extent, it aims to work in each parish in connection with the parish church. Its membership numbers nearly one hundred and twenty-five thousand women and girls of every rank in England alone, and its operations are extended to Scotland, Ireland, and the colonies. Its aims, as stated in the Constitution, are :

"1st. To bind together in one society, ladies as *associates*, and working - girls as *members* for mutual help (both religious and secular), for sympathy and for prayer.

"2d. To encourage purity of life, dutifulness to parents, faithfulness to employers, and thrift.

"3d. To provide the privileges of the society for its members wherever they may be by giving them an introduction from one branch to another."

The following are the central rules :

"1st. Associates to be members of the Church of England (there is no such restriction as to members), and the organization to follow as much as possible that of the Church, being diocesan, ruridecanal, and parochial.

"2d. Associates and members to contribute annually to the funds : the former not less than 2s. 6d. a year, the latter not less than 6d., the members' payment to go to the central fund.

"3d. No girl that has not borne a virtuous character to be admitted as a member."

"The third rule," says Lady Shrewsbury, "is the

hinge on which the whole society hangs. The advantages and privileges afforded to the members are to make virtue easier and to act as a fence between them and the pitfalls of vice. That numberless and strong fences are necessary is certain. And that these fences must surround our girls from an early age is, without doubt, a necessity of the age. The Girls' Friendly Society recognizes this, and endeavors within the limited powers of its comparatively few workers to supply this want. At eight years old little girls are received as candidates and trained to be dutiful to their parents, and modest in conduct; and at twelve they are passed into the society as members, in which condition they remain until marriage gives them a husband's protection."

The privileges of the society are these :

"1st. Every girl has a right to go to the associate as a friend for sympathy, advice, and help."

In case of emigration, she is watched over until she reaches her destination, being safely placed upon her vessel when leaving England, and received at the docks by special agents when she lands in America or the colonies. Emigration is not, however, encouraged by the society.

2d. There are "lodges" for these girls in the metropolis, and most of the large towns whither they flock for employment. "These lodges take the place of home, and are under the supervision of a lady superintendent or matron who 'mothers' the inmates." Charges for board are made proportionate to the earnings of the inmates. Games and amusements are provided, instruction is given, friendships are formed, and a home-life cultivated whose attractions are strong enough to keep them from the temptations without.

No element in the society's life and work is found to be more useful and is more highly appreciated than that of the attachments that grow up between the girls and the ladies who care for them. And another feature scarcely less valuable is that of the deep and lasting friendships that are formed among the members.

The society extends its influence into the various occupations where girls are employed, and manages the different branches of its work by means of eight separate departments. There is a department for members in professions and business, which includes work among school-mistresses, students, pupil-teachers, shop-girls, and dress-makers; a department for members in mills and factories; for candidates from workhouses and orphanages; for members in service (domestic servants cannot, however, belong to the society or attend its meetings without the permission of their mistresses); a department for lodges and lodgings; a department for literature (which publishes a journal for associates, and two magazines for members, besides books and pamphlets); a department for sick members, and homes of rest; and a department for domestic economy and industrial training, which trains children for domestic service, and instructs members by lecture and otherwise to earn their own living.

The Church of England performs many grateful services for the poor by the hands of *deaconesses and sisters of mercy.* The sisters live in communities, take vows of celibacy, and usually make the devotional life the chief object of their seclusion from the world. They usually belong to the extreme high-church party. A deaconess, on the other hand, is a person set apart by a bishop for religious work. The bearers of this office take no vows, may be married or single, and need not necessarily live in a religious community. Many, if not most, of them are of the low-church party.

Both classes are largely engaged in Christian and benevolent work, and are frequently employed in connection with the parish church under the direction of its incumbent. These women, protected by a distinctive dress, visit the low parts of the city without danger, penetrate the dark and loathsome dwellings of the very poorest people, and search out the destitute sick, to whom their ministries bring the greatest comfort. Mothers are taught to take proper care of their children; hints and instruction as to nursing are given to the friends and relatives of invalids, and free nurses are supplied in cases of extreme need. The sisters and deaconesses, being trained nurses, are able, by their constant presence in the sick-chamber, to do more for the sufferer, especially when he is in destitute circumstances, than any physician could do through occasional visits.

In England, as in our own land, it is not easy to secure Sunday-school teachers who are really efficient and competent to instruct the children placed under their charge. Here, too, the services of women of this order are extremely valuable and effective. They also conduct week-day schools, ragged-schools, and industrial schools. Orphanages have been established and maintained by them, as well as temporary homes for missionaries, houses of mercy for penitents, day nurseries, refuges, homes for incurables and for convalescents. There is a party of sisters which appears every day at noon among the rough laborers, at the docks of East London, bringing trucks loaded with food and hot coffee, which is sold at nominal prices. Thus they hope to win away patronage from the drinking-places that cluster thickly about the dock-gates. They are also largely engaged in hospital and infirmary work. Several hospitals for women and children have been established by them, and the nursing at other hospitals is entirely under their charge.

There is a notable tendency among earnest people of every name and order in England to establish as many points of contact as possible between the church and the daily life of the people. This tendency is illustrated by the extent to which *friendly societies* and *workingmen's clubs* are encouraged. It had formerly been the case, and is still, to some extent, that such institutions held their meetings in halls connected with public-houses, which the publicans were glad to provide, rent free, for the sake of their presence and incidental patronage. This practice is common in the United States also. Such institutions have, in many cases, been provided with quarters of their own largely through the donations of benevolent men, and under the auspices of the churches. Mission-halls, chapels, school-rooms, and other buildings of the sort have also been thrown open to their use. It is a common thing for gentlemen of high standing to belong to them, and to attend their meetings. And they frequently elect prominent clergymen and others to the office of president.

One of the great national sins of England is that of intemperance. In this respect there is a marked contrast between the British and continental cities. The drinking-places in London are more numerous, are usually of a lower class, and deal in liquors that are more injurious than those most commonly drank at

Paris and Berlin;* drunkenness is more frequent. In the dingy, foul, crowded, poverty-stricken parts, where human existence is fullest of misery, the gin-palaces stand in tawdry splendor on every corner, like shining parasites fattened on the life-blood of the poor. Perhaps there is no more drunkenness among men than some of our own cities exhibit, and there is certainly more excuse for it, if miserable homes, costly food, and cheap drink can constitute an excuse. But the drunkenness of women, that may be seen in the poorer parts of London, is peculiarly shocking to a stranger. Women of the lower classes appear to be almost as frequent patrons of the gin-shops as their husbands.† As one passes the open doors of the public-houses any summer night in East London, he can see large numbers of them drinking at public bars, with babies in their arms, and small children hanging about their skirts. Since drunkenness is even more demoralizing in the case of the woman and mother than in that of the father of the household, its ill-effects among the London poor are simply incalculable. Corresponding with the extent and virulence of the disease have been the strength of the remedies put forth to meet it. The temperance movement is remarkably powerful throughout all England; so much so that official statistics show an encouraging diminution of drunkenness during the last few years, as well as a decrease of government revenues from taxes upon intoxicants. Among the

---

* We do not mean to imply that either of those cities is a model in this respect.

† This may be, to some extent, due to the custom of employing bar-maids. The presence of a woman in a drinking-place makes it a shade more respectable for other women to visit.

working-classes, with whom the movement has taken its firmest hold, multitudes of temperance societies have sprung up. Many of these combine with their temperance work a scheme of insurance against sickness and death, and are known as *temperance friendly societies.*

All religious work among the lower classes is shot through and through with temperance. In the case of many, sin of every sort has become so interwoven and identified with the drink passion that this is the sin of sins to them, and they talk about the Christian life as though they considered it to be chiefly a deliverance by the grace of God from the power of strong drink, combined with a commission to work for the salvation of others from the same bondage. Many of the churches, both those of the Establishment and of Nonconformists, employ reformed men as special temperance missionaries to devote themselves exclusively to this line of work.

The Church of England Temperance Society has its branches in almost every parish of the English cities. It includes a Woman's Union and a Juvenile Union. It publishes several papers and conducts special departments for police-court work, for railway work, for army work, for work among cabmen, 'busmen, and others; in connection with this and kindred movements among the Nonconformists multitudes of cocoa and coffee taverns have been established throughout the whole country, twelve hundred and forty-four of which are now known to be in operation.

Brave work has been and is being done in England, in battling with the fury of the social evil. The life-struggle of a crowded city like London greatly aggra-

vates and inflames the temptations consequent upon
such passions as flesh is heir to. For a young man to
get foothold in any line of business requires a long,
hard struggle. Marriage is late and uncertain. The
horrors of the one-room life blot out all sense of mod-
esty in early childhood from thousands of daughters of
the poor, and want continually tempting them to pros-
titution and finding the defences against such temptation weakened or destroyed, fills the street with fallen
women. The work of *the White Cross movement* is well
known in the United States, and many branches of that
organization have already been planted upon our shores.
It is not a denominational movement, but includes
in its ranks men of all sects and parties. There is a
Church of England Purity Society, which works in the
same line and is practically the same thing. These
societies aim to promote purity among men, a chival-
rous respect for womanhood, prevention of the young
from contamination, rescue work, and a higher tone of
public opinion. Their membership is confined to men
above eighteen years of age and their meetings are for
men only.

In order to show how these and other branches of
Christian activity are woven together in the life of the
most energetic London churches, a brief account will
be given of the work of two or three who are directly
dealing with the problem of reaching the working-
classes.

Our first example is *St. Anne's, Limehouse.* This
church is situated far down in the East End, a part of
London which visitors and the more prosperous portion
of the Londoners themselves never see unless, perhaps,
from the windows of a railway carriage as their train

hurries them over a long viaduct that crosses that region.

The parish, no part of which is more than ten minutes' walk from the church, embraces a population of something more than ten thousand. It is composed chiefly of artisans, lodging-house keepers, sailors and dock laborers, many of the latter being very poor. There are about twenty manufacturers and tradesfolk of the wealthier sort, but with these exceptions persons so engaged in that neighborhood reside far away from their place of business. There are also two streets of small shop-keepers of the lower-middle class. The church has on its parochial staff four resident clergymen, one Scripture-reader, ninety-two Sunday-school teachers, fourteen day-school teachers, choir-master, organist, twenty choir-men, forty choir-boys, two trained nurses, two mission women, twelve district visitors, and one temperance missionary. The choir-boys are paid one penny for each week-day attendance.

The church has a seating capacity of thirteen hundred. There are three mission-rooms, the first of which seats four hundred, the second eighty, the third forty. Four services are held in the church on every Sunday : holy communion at eight A.M., morning service at eleven A.M., followed twice in the month by a second celebration of the holy communion. At three o'clock a congregational Bible-class is held, there are baptisms at four, and evening prayer at seven. Two services, morning and evening prayer, are held in the church on every day in the week and twice during the week—the evening service includes a sermon ; besides which there are many extra services on feast days and other special occasions.

Mission-room No. 1 has a Sunday-school on Sunday morning, another in the afternoon, and a ragged Sunday-school in the evening, besides Bible-classes for young men and for young women. During the four Monday evenings of the month the room is used for the successive meetings of three communicants' guilds: one for adults, one for young men, and one for young women, and a branch of the Church of England Purity Society. Tuesday afternoon there is a mothers' meeting in this place; Tuesday evening, a sewing-class for girls; Wednesday, a second mothers' meeting, and Wednesday evening a ragged-school Band of Hope. Thursday evening there is a Sunday-school Band of Hope, followed by an adult temperance meeting, and Friday evening the room is occupied by a friendly society.

Mission-room No. 2 has a Bible-class for men on every Sunday, with an enrolled membership numbering one hundred and sixteen, and an average attendance of fifty-five, and a class about half as large for girls. At the same place there are held, in the course of the week, a mothers' meeting, a men's night-school, a lady's Bible-reading, a children's service, a Gospel service, a woman's Bible-class, a social evening for boys, a social evening for girls, including a working-party, library, penny bank, etc., and a general prayer-meeting. All these meetings are conducted by deaconesses from Mildmay Park Institute.

In connection with mission-room No. 3 there are out-of-door services on every Sunday evening from June to October, followed by mission services within. There is also a special meeting for boys on Sunday afternoon, and in the course of the week there are two social evenings for men, and one for girls.

At the same time the National School * buildings are utilized by this most active church for the following meetings :—Sunday morning a Sunday-school for boys, Sunday afternoon a Sunday-school for girls; also four Bible-classes, one for men, one for young men, one for lads, and one for girls. There is in this building a weekly teachers' meeting, a penny savings bank, and a library for all the Sunday-schools. In addition to all these, there are regular weekly services held three times every week in neighboring factories during the dinner hour.

Every year this church has confirmations, for which preparatory instruction is given to catechumens in nine weekly classes during three months preceding that service. In the way of guilds and societies, there are reported a missionary society, a communicants' society, a maternity society, a Church of England temperance society, three Bands of Hope, a Sunday-school and missionary-box society. In the line of recreations, etc., the church provides weekly social evenings for factory-hands, a sewing-class for the ragged-school, temperance entertainments, meetings for boys and young men, quarterly teas for young men's and young women's Bible-classes, cricket, football, and swimming clubs, country walking-parties, annual excursions for the choir and Sunday-school, and confirmation anniversaries.

Another large East London church, *St. Mary's, Whitechapel,* has on its parochial staff a rector and three assistant curates, one Scripture-reader, and three city missionaries, one of whom works exclusively among the

---

* The " National Schools " are church schools. The " Board Schools " are those supported by the State.

Jews; a mission-woman, a nurse for sick poor, and five licensed lay readers, besides church - wardens, choir, Sunday-school teachers, etc. Open-air meetings are held five evenings during the week throughout six months of the year. It has a stone pulpit built into the exterior wall of the church, from which wayside hearers may be addressed. The list of clubs, societies, entertainments, and enterprises of various sorts that it sustains is even more extensive than that already quoted. It includes a clothing-club in five branches, with a membership of eight hundred and thirty-nine; a sick and burial society, cricket-club, swimming-club, lawn tennis-club, young men's association, branches of the Church of England Temperance Society, both for adults and children, with weekly meetings and entertainments ; a girls' friendly society, a children's country-holiday fund, a destitute children's dinner society, an emigration fund, an oriental coffee-house, an industrial home, a registry for domestic servants, a tonic sol-fa class, a chess class, a parish magazine with a circulation of seven hundred, Christmas treats, summer excursions, concerts, magic - lantern exhibitions, soup-kitchen, and branches of the White Cross Army.

There is another East London church, whose work being somewhat exceptional in character, is worthy of special attention and study. This is *St. Jude's, White-chapel.* Its parish is occupied by workingmen, small shop-keepers, and clerks, and, although the region may not be quite so miserable as that which surrounds St. Anne's, the fact of its proximity to "Rag Fair " and the famous " Petticoat Lane," that once was, is evidence enough that it is none too respectable. The church is not a large one, and except for the character of its vicar, would not be of special importance. The latter, the Rev. Samuel A. Barnett, is one of the most radical members of the broad-church party, and a well-known writer on social and industrial questions. He is a man of great personal attractions, of commanding influence, is bold in his thinking, positive in his convictions, and extremely radical in many of his positions. No one can doubt the depth and genuineness of his sympathy with the poor, for whose relief he spends his life in plans and labors along somewhat original lines.

In the regular work of St. Jude's church some of the more common and generally approved methods of religious effort are discarded. They declined, for example, to join in the mission which was conducted by other churches in the vicinity on the ground that such movements are of doubtful value, often productive of incidental evil so great as to more than counterbalance the good that results from them, and also on the ground that they foster a type of religion in which the people are already well instructed, namely, a religion of sentiments and fears, while they fail to develop what the poor stand in greatest need of,—a religion of manliness and culture. The common plan of visiting the poor in their homes is not extensively practiced by the people of St. Jude's, for it is held that such visits tend to rob them of their self-respect.

Among the special features of the work in this place the following are noted :

1st. The church is open every day, from 11 A.M. until 5 P.M., "for those who would pray, read, and think in quietness."

2d. The regular Sunday morning service is broken into three short services by slight pauses between the morning prayer, sermon, and litany, because "after a week's work many cannot rise until late in the day and to few is it given to be able to restrain their thoughts for more than half an hour at a time."

3d. The church is made attractive at all times by the presence of flowers and appropriate works of art. A bright Venetian mosaic and a beautiful drinking fountain with suitable inscriptions adorn its exterior front.

4th. There is a so-called "worship hour" after Sunday-evening service which seems to be mainly devoted to music, meditation, and silent prayer.

5th. Unusual attention is given to matters of secular instruction. Night-schools are held throughout the week ; there are special classes in such subjects as French, science, and violin; a popular-ballad class meets once a week. During the summer, various classes take the form of rambling clubs and devote their excursions to the study of geology, botany, and architecture.

6th There is a lending-library with about a thousand volumes which are kept in constant circulation.

7th. But the feature in the work at St. Jude's which is most unique of all is the institution of an *annual free exhibition of fine art* for the benefit of the working-people of East London. It is held in the rooms of the school-building which stands closely beside the church, is open every year at Easter and continues open day and evening seven days in the week for about one month. The pictures and other objects displayed are of a very high class and loaned from the best houses in London. This is held to be a matter of extreme importance and indeed essential to the purpose for which the exhibition was inaugurated, its object being to elevate the taste, and through the taste, the whole nature

9

of the people by constantly placing before them what is really excellent until familiarity has taught them to know it so well that they can instantly choose between the good and vicious. This year the exhibition contained some five hundred paintings, several of which had been leading pictures at different times in the Royal Academy. It was pronounced the finest exhibition of modern paintings that could be seen at the time in the whole metropolis. An elaborate catalogue, containing not only the titles of the pictures, but simple, well-worded comments and explanations, with extracts from Mr. Ruskin and the poets, was sold for a penny. There was also a number of ladies and gentlemen in constant attendance to act, not only as custodians of the valuable property, but also as guides and interpreters to the poorer and more inexperienced visitors. The exhibition was first opened in the spring of 1880, and the number of visitors that year was about twelve thousand. With each successive season it has become more popular, until last year, when it was visited by fifty-six thousand people, three-fourths of whom were mechanics, artisans, and laborers. Regarding this enterprise Mr. Barnett writes :

"The inability of those who constitute the majority of the nation to understand even the language of some of the best modern teachers. reveals the condition to which society has been brought in the pursuit of wealth. It also suggests means of reform. The people must be made familiar with pictures and books. They must learn the language of thought, as language is always learned by familiarity. Galleries and libraries should thus be conveniently placed and opened at fitting times. Sunday cannot be an unfit day on which to become familiar with the language of pictures and books,—the language through which God has often come to men." *

Another institution deserves our notice in this connection, which, although quite distinct from St. Jude's church, stands beside it, and is undoubtedly an outgrowth of the life and thinking of its vicar. This is styled *The University Extension Society.* It is composed of a dozen or twenty young men, including churchmen, nonconformists, and even unbelievers, all of them university graduates, who, feeling the grievousness of the evils springing from the growing gulf between rich and poor, are bent upon doing something, all that is within their power, toward bridging it over. They have accordingly come down to live among the people of the East End, have joined workingmen's clubs, and have endeavored in every possible way to identify themselves with the life of that portion of the town which is almost exclusively occupied by the children of toil.

Their house of residence, called the "Settlement," closely resembles an ordinary college building in its internal arrangements. There is a comfortable dining-room, a spacious and attractive drawing-room, there are several convenient class-rooms, and there are small parlors and tiny bedrooms for about twenty men. In connection with the settlement there is a good-sized audience-room, called Toynbee Hall, where courses of free lectures for workingmen are given by eminent men of science and letters every winter. The members of the society are most of them engaged in the law-courts and in other parts of the city during the day. In the

---

* For other examples of parochial work see *Official Year-Book of the Church of England*, London, 1886, pp. 46–55.

evening, besides taking a part in their various clubs, they teach selected classes of young men in their own rooms or the class-rooms at the settlement. The members of these classes are brought together in weekly social evenings in the great drawing-room. Lady friends from the West End are generally present upon these occasions, and contribute music and selected readings as well as their society to the entertainment; and there has been an effort to secure also the presence of the wives and sisters of the workingmen. But this, it is said, has not yet been successfully accomplished, much to the annoyance and perplexity of the young reformers The movement, while not distinctively religious, is far from being irreligious. Its primary aim seems to be to extend to those whose hard, laborious life-struggle has entirely cut them off from it, some of the fruits of Christianity which take the shape of intellectual and æsthetic culture.

The organization is but a new one, and the methods thus far necessarily tentative and experimental. There is a growing conviction among its members, as we are informed, that little can be done to help the workingmen without the powerful alliance of religion. Sects and sectarianism stand in their way, being there and everywhere the greatest practical hindrance to effective Christian work. Some of them at least are, therefore, driven for relief to the extreme position of those who with Mr. Barnett would make the Church "truly national"—"the nation organized for worship," and every Englishman—be he Churchman, Nonconformist, Turk or infidel—a member of it, with a voice in the control of its affairs.

A style of work in some, though not in all respects,

similar to that of the " University Extension Society," is being done by a colony of Oxford graduates, whose headquarters are known as the *Oxford House*, St. Andrew Parish, Bethnal Green. These men are usually students of divinity who, having taken their degree, spend a year in Christian work in London before ordination, as a sort of post-graduate course of preparation for their life-service. The region is one of the most miserable in the whole city. Besides engaging in house-to-house visitation and general mission work, these Oxford men have organized a number of clubs for workingmen and for boys, which differ from the ordinary workingmen's clubs in being strictly temperance organizations. They have also conducted a lecture bureau, designed to furnish free lectures of instructive character for workingmen's clubs. In prosecuting this enterprise they have been able to secure the services of about twenty lecturers during the past winter, mostly Oxford men and specialists, and they have sent each of them out to address audiences of workingmen three or four times in the course of the last winter.

The neighborhood of Bethnal Green is occupied by multitudes of poor artisans that are engaged in various kinds of handicraft. The competition of machines and factories has of late years made their slow and laborious methods of work extremely unremunerative; in consequence of which many are reduced to penury. Yet most of the productions of these people have the peculiar beauty, strength, and excellence of hand-made goods. Hundreds of the original Huguenot family which live there are, for example, still engaged in weaving with hand-looms in their homes, the heavy, old-fashioned, costly silks of former times. The Oxford men, feeling that if the character of this work were more generally known, and its excellence understood and appreciated, there would be a ready market for it, have set on foot arrangements for the great industrial exhibition of the manufactures of East London, the so-called " East Enderies," which was recently opened by Lady Rosebery, assisted by Lord Lorne, under most favorable auspices and with every promise of success. In this way they hope to provide a ready sale for the manufactures of their poor neighbors, and thus to promote greater prosperity among them.

CHAPTER V.

In discussing the work of the dissenting churches in London we shall find that many of the methods employed by them are so similar to those already mentioned that they need no further description. It should not, however, on that account be inferred that they are practiced with less earnestness and success by the nonconformists than by churchmen.

The dissenting churches have about seven hundred places of worship, of all sorts, in London. Three hundred and thirty of these, most of which are quite small, belong to various bodies of Wesleyans and Methodists; one hundred and twelve to Independents or Congregationalists; ninety-nine to Baptists; sixty-seven to Presbyterians; and eighty or ninety to a variety of smaller sects and to undenominational missions.

The ordinary services of these churches are arranged and conducted in all essential respects like those of our own country. There are, however, some slight differences between their ways and ours, which are perhaps worth noticing. The religious services are, if we are not mistaken, considerably more frequent than is usual among us. It is common to have two prayer-meetings on Sunday, besides two regular church services and Sunday-school. Not a few of the churches have two sessions of the Sunday-school, the first coming before church in the morning, the second in the afternoon, and even have the same officers, pupils, and teachers at both sessions. Their Sunday-schools, as a rule, have more the character of mission schools than ours, and are usually not attended by the children of the best families in the church. Yet some schools are conducted on the American plan. Many churches have a separate service for children going on at the same time with the regular morning service. It is a common plan to hold two prayer-meetings on week-days ; one, perhaps, on Monday and one on Saturday evening; and a more formal service with preaching on Wednesday or Thursday evening.

The order of worship varies considerably in different churches, but most of them agree in certain particulars: there are usually two Scripture lessons, one from the Old Testament and one from the New; there is almost always more singing than is common with us; morning service in many of the churches includes, at least, four hymns and a chant, or three hymns, an anthem, and a chant. It was noticed in two prominent Congregational churches in London that, during a morning service followed by a brief communion service, there were sung, always by choir and congregation together, an anthem, two chants, and five hymns. A brief prayer often immediately precedes the sermon. It is a universal custom among the English people upon taking their seat in church or any religious meeting to bow the head or kneel in silent prayer, and also to remain for a moment in the attitude of devotion after the closing benediction. The pews are supplied with Bibles as well as hymn-books, and the majority of the congregation follow the preacher in his reading with open Bible, and look up the text.

The celebration of the Lord's Supper is rather more frequent in most of the churches than is common with us, the event occurring as often as once and even twice each month. In the latter case there is usually one celebration after a morning, and one after an evening service, in order that it may suit the convenience of all to be present at least once every month. They have a pleasant custom of seating the deacons upon the platform about the pastor during the celebration of the feast. There is also a system of tickets by which the members of the church indicate their presence at the sacramental service. Each member present deposits a dated and numbered ticket in the collection-box with the offering for the poor. This does not mean that no member can commune without a ticket; the ticket is simply an indication of his presence, and enables the church clerk to keep a roll of attendance—a very useful thing, especially where the congregation includes a large number of poor and obscure persons.* Strangers are most cordially welcomed to the Lord's table in all the churches, the Baptist as well as others, and are even invited to assist in the sacramental service.

Most of the methods of evangelistic work carried on by the dissenting churches closely resemble our own. They have prayer-meetings, inquiry-rooms, Gospel services, and protracted meetings precisely like ours. Although the music used for regular church services is

---

* We cannot say that this is a universal custom, but only that it is a common one. We trust our readers will not forget that we claim in none of these matters to speak with authority except within the range of a very limited experience.

somewhat unfamiliar, in evangelistic meetings of all kinds one invariably hears the well-known songs introduced by Mr. Bliss and Mr. Sankey; and, much as these simple melodies may be despised on artistic grounds, they certainly have a remarkable adaptation to the work for which they were designed, that of evangelistic services among common people. They are used in such meetings not only in London and all over England and Scotland, but at the McAll mission in Paris and the Young Men's Christian Association in Berlin.

Having premised thus much in general, brief description will be given of the work of two or three dissenting churches which deal directly with the problem of evangelizing the masses.

The first example is that of the *Highbury Quadrant Congregational Church*, of which Dr. Llewellyn D. Bevan, formerly of New York and lately removed to Melbourne, Australia, was pastor at the time it was visited by the writer. This church stands in the midst of a rather prosperous district in one of the newer parts of London. The comfortable-looking houses about it are occupied by people of the middle and upper-middle classes. There are poorer neighborhoods, however, within a few minutes' walk, inhabited by working-people. The church is but eight years old, and its commodious house of worship has been completed only about five years. Yet, although so young, it already has two thriving missions. The relation of one of these missions to the parent church gives an extremely valuable hint at the way religious work may be successfully sustained and vigorously pushed in the poorest neighborhoods.

The mission church of Britannia Row is nearly a mile and a half away from the parent church. It stands in a narrow lane off from a portion of a great North London thoroughfare, to which its abandoned character has given the title, "The Devil's Mile." The population thereabout is of the poorest class,—day-laborers, wash-women, and costermongers. The mission has all the appointments of a regular church. Its house of worship is large and comfortable. It has a spacious Sunday-school room and class-rooms below the main auditorium, a pipe organ, and the usual church furnishings. A regular pastor, whom nature and experience have combined to give peculiar fitness for such work, devotes his whole time and strength to its service. It has its own treasurer, deacons, and committees, and is in all respects like an ordinary church except that it leans upon a stronger sister for support.

No church in such a community with such a membership could live a vigorously independent life, if it could live independently at all. There would be two great difficulties, and these the chief difficulties that disturb independent religious enterprises everywhere in poor neighborhoods : First, lack of money to support an efficient pastor and to conduct the affairs of the church in a proper way ; second, lack of workers competent to take helpful part in prayer-meetings, to organize and lead the various religious, literary, and benevolent societies that are needed to lift along the work, and to teach in the Sunday-school. In this case the difficulty is overcome by uniting the weak church with a strong one. The latter, out of its abundance, supplies the needs of the former and both are benefited by the transaction,—one with the blessing of giving, the other with that of receiving. The Highbury Quadrant people pay the entire pastor's salary for their brethren at Britannia Row, and in hard times when the weather is bitter and work short, so that many are in destitution, they come generously to their aid with gifts of food, clothing, and fuel. The stronger church sends also a corps of its very best workers to assist in the Sunday-school and prayer-meetings, to lead mothers' meetings, and even to take the office of deacon in the church. It would be strange if this outlay of its strength in support of a feeble sister did not, as it does, react powerfully upon the sustaining church, giving it more means for home expenditure and more workers for home work. It would be strange if going down to play the part of brother and sister in deed and in truth, by working shoulder to shoulder with these sons of toil and daughters of sorrow, did not, as it does, give to the well-to-do people of the Quadrant church such an understanding of the needs of the poor, and such sympathy with their troubles, as no end of reading and speculation could afford. It would be strange if these gifts of money, of strength, and of fellowship did not soften the bitterness of the poor toward the rich, as indeed it does, convince them of the reality of Christian brotherhood and open their hearts to all the uplifting influences of the Christian religion. Within the past ten years the neighborhood of Britannia Row has been surprisingly transformed. Neat and comfortable dwellings are rapidly taking the place of the wretched rookeries that once abounded in those parts. Where once the people were almost without exception ragged, drunken, and miserable, they now appear in a great majority of cases to be neatly

clothed and comfortably situated. This remarkable
change is doubtless chiefly due to the influence of the
mission church.

The other mission connected with the Highbury Quadrant church is smaller and more of the usual type. The
feature of it that appeared to the writer most interesting was a workingman's club and benefit society, comprising some seven hundred members, of which Dr.
Bevan was president, for whose meetings the mission
buildings are used. A similar club meets also in the
lecture-room of the main church. The church, with
both of its missions, sustains a very great number of
societies, clubs, classes, meetings, penny banks, unions,
mothers' meetings, fathers' meetings, etc. The church
report states that " irrespective of meetings for worship,
there are in all, not less than 56 such institutions, all of
which, with the exception of five, meet at least once a
week, that honor the pastor with the title of president.
The Sunday-school scholars in all these institutions
number more than 1,300. The members of the various
mothers' meetings nearly 1,000. Their annual contributions for the purchase of coal and clothing exceed
£600 ; penny banks have 926 depositors and their total
deposits last year amounted to £579. The various
temperance organizations have a membership of 700.
The mutual benefit societies under various names, a
membership of over 1,100, with an income for mutual
help of more than £1,350. Once a week during six
months of the year about 350 poor children receive a
meat dinner, and 700 poor families or 3,500 individuals
receive on Christmas eve sufficient material to provide
substantial dinners for two days."

Not far away from the church are the stables of one

of the great street railway companies. In these buildings, and on the cars that run out from them, are employed, day and night, seven days in the week, a large
number of men of a class as much neglected by teachers of religion as any in civilized countries. A missionary is employed for their special benefit; a man of their
own rank, who, before his conversion, was well known
to them as a famous quack, gamester, and drunken
horse-doctor. He is now a thoroughly changed man,
full of zeal, and a rough sort of power, and an ardent
advocate of temperance. His history, experience, and
natural gifts, sanctified by the grace of God, secure for
him great influence over the men. He has won scores
and hundreds of them to total abstinence, and many to
the service of Christ.

It is estimated that through these various channels,
the church, whose membership is only 517, comes in
contact with at least 10,000 lives.

The *Tolmer's Square Congregational Church* adapts
its work to the needs of the poorer classes by a very interesting movement of a somewhat different character.
This church stands in the northwest quarter of London,
not far from the junction of Euston and Tottenham
Court Roads. The neighborhood is one which was
long since abandoned by the wealthy, and from which
well-to-do householders have gradually been moving
away, leaving the better streets to business and boarding-houses, while the poorer ones swarm with an ever
denser population of artisans and laborers. Few
churches have been called upon to look more squarely
in the face the sternest, most difficult problems of city
evangelization. As an effort toward the solution of
those problems, some ten years ago, under the pastor-

ate of the Rev. Henry Simon, now of Westminster chapel, there was projected by this church an institute for workingmen; that is, a place for the meetings and the headquarters of their friendly and temperance societies, and a place where they could always gather for a social evening. The Rev. Arthur Hall, of Bristol, brother of Dr. Newman Hall, succeeded Mr. Simon, and pushed forward with great energy the plans of his predecessor. During his pastorate that noble building was completed which bears the name of *Tolmer Institute.* At a distance of about three minutes' walk from the church, it rises loftily in the midst of a multitude of small shops, gleaming gin-palaces, and dingy tenement-houses. Four shops occupy the ground floor, one of which is a temperance café belonging to the institute. The rest of the building is occupied by rooms of various shapes and sizes, carefully adapted to its needs. Among these are a gymnasium and three good-sized audience-rooms, the largest of which has seats for 800 people. The cost of the whole establishment, together with the land on which it stands, was not far from £14,000. Not more than five years have elapsed since its completion, and about three since the coming of the present pastor, the Rev. Frederic Hastings. Yet under his skillful management it has become a potent centre of Christian influence in that community, and its spacious accommodations are already taxed to their utmost capacity.

Among the various institutions for working-people that meet in this place the following are noted: A Sunday-school, a Band of Hope, two lodges of Good Templars, and one of Sons of Temperance, a Woman's Temperance Society, a Thrift Society, three Building

Societies, a Mutual Improvement Society, a "Help My-self" Society, two Phœnix (that is, temperance friendly) Societies, a Penny Bank, and a number of evening classes. There are also frequent "smoking concerts" for workingmen, and popular penny concerts, which draw audiences of seven or eight hundred every Saturday night, and pay their way handsomely. Here the pastor's wife holds mothers' meetings, where from seventy-five to one hundred poor women gather weekly, bringing their babies and their sewing, to hear reading, music, and gentle words of encouragement and helpfulness. Here, too, are held frequent mission prayer-meetings. The writer attended one of them on a Sunday evening after church. The room, which was not a small one, was completely filled with people of the humbler sort, and a depth of feeling and spiritual power was manifest in the assembly such as one rarely meets. The leader that night chanced to be a woman. She filled her office with such grace and dignity, and spoke so fittingly, that we afterward learned with surprise that she was only a cook in a noble lady's family. That cook has gathered about herself a band of young women who meet every week for prayer and Bible study. She also gives her services most wisely and efficiently to other branches of Christian work, and is thus exerting an influence for good which is probably equalled by that of few noble ladies in England or in any other country. The best thing about it is, that all these various institutions move on of themselves, and are not a great and crushing weight upon the shoulders of the pastor. The friendly and temperance societies pay rent for their privileges. The café is a means of income, and these, together with the rents of the shops and other revenues, render the institute very nearly self-supporting. All the meetings are intrusted to the management of certain committees, which appoint their leaders, and are responsible for their conduct. The minister attends only so many of the score and more of weekly meetings as he finds time for. All is so skillfully arranged that he can be absent from the parish for months at a time without the occurrence of any confusion in its internal workings.

It is worthy of notice that the chief political power in that district, low and vicious as the neighborhood appears, is in the hands of no brewer nor liquor-dealer. The member of Parliament for the west division of St. Pancreas publicly acknowledged at the last election that he owed his seat to the personal influence of Mr. Hastings. This influence is doubtless largely due to the quick wit and fiery eloquence of the man. But it is not improbable that his relation to Tolmer Institute is his weightiest argument in winning to the cause he advocated the votes and confidence of the people.

Before leaving this part of the subject, the reader will be introduced to one other church, engaged in work of still another type among the poor—work which, in its way, is as remarkable as any that the world has to show. This is the *East London Tabernacle.* Its pastor, the Rev. Archibald G. Brown, is a Baptist of the broad, English type. He is a man of rather striking appearance, somewhat above middle height, rather slender, with soldierly bearing and laic dress, is prematurely gray, with a fresh, animated face, clear tenor voice, and eyes that are full of leadership. He is gifted with remarkable executive capacity, and is at the same time a ready and effective speaker, filled with a passion-

10

ate love for souls.* His audiences surpass in size any that we saw in London, with the exception of Mr. Spurgeon's and those of the cathedrals. The church is a plain square building, with scarcely the appearance of an ecclesiastical structure. It has seats for thirty-two hundred people, and remarkably good acoustic properties. It stands on Burdett Road, a few rods from Mile End Road, in the centre of East London. There is probably nowhere else in the world so extensive and so homogeneous a population of working-people as that in whose midst it is located. Many of these people are exceedingly poor and degraded. Within five minutes' walk of the church, in several directions, one may come upon the lowest types of human habitation. It was in this neighborhood, and by the assistance of Mr. Brown and his missionaries, that many of the investigations were made, the account of which, under the title " The Bitter Cry of Outcast London," so startled England and all the world four years ago. In many of these streets there are not, on the average, two rooms to each family of inhabitants. In some houses there are as many families as rooms; and such rooms, small, dark, foul, and miserable beyond description!

A correspondent of *The Daily Telegraph* has written a graphic account of an interview with Mr. Brown and a visit to certain parts of his parish, from which we quote at length in order to give a better conception of the nature of the work in which he is engaged:

" If you want statistics of the one-room horror you shall have them out of my very district," said the

---

* This is chosen as an example of a style of Christian work such as that of Mr. Spurgeon, Dr. Bernado, and others, in which the personality of the leader is a most important element.

minister, turning to a carefully prepared tabulated
sheet, which comprised every house to which his missionaries had access; "what do you say to this? three
hundred and forty rooms yield nearly two hundred and
sixty families; or in square figures, twelve hundred
and forty-four human beings. Cast your eye, sir, over
the list. Number — Cable Street, there are six families in twelve rooms, and twenty-nine persons living
in the twelve-roomed house. Next door there are
twenty-eight human beings in the house, exactly the
same size. Number — B—— Street appears to head
the list. No less than forty-seven human beings, the
total of six families, are thrust every night into six
rooms, and you shall presently see what rooms they
are, for which sums varying from 2s. 6d. to 3s. 6d. are
charged—rooms with ceilings breaking away from the
rafters; smoky and grimy rooms; rooms where chimneys smoke and windows won't unfasten; rooms smoth-
ered in vermin, or overrun with mice; rooms approached
by breakneck staircases as black as pitch, garrets of
rooms with sloping rafters; cellars of rooms underneath the pavement; rooms overlooking low, miserable
streets or foul mud-yards; hopeless, cheerless, despairing rooms where wives strip their children piecemeal
for the pawn-shop; where the furniture seldom consists of more than a broken table or backless chair;
where the children, when a stranger knocks at the door,
come across to him with starving eyes, and ask, 'Have
you brought mother some bread?' and where the
blind, neglected, lonely widow sits upon an empty floor
in a fireless room, during the dull November day, and
mumbles hopeless assent when asked by the good-
hearted missionary to join him in prayer to God that

some miracle may be worked in order to lighten this unspeakable darkness." *

The reporter thus describes some of the places as he himself saw them in company with the missionary:

"We go from bad to worse. Elizabeth Court is infinitely more foul than James Place, and the poverty more heart-rending. A widow has just managed to screw together one pennyworth of coals, and she expresses her thankfulness enthusiastically, for at last she has got one shirt to wash and perhaps this may mean a beginning of work again. But what a room in which to wash a shirt! The furniture broken, the walls grimy, the floor filthy, the bedding of that indescribable color between brown and black.

"We ascend to a garret. An Irish woman is here in despair. She has pawned almost the whole of her available property already. At home with her are an idiot son, a daughter of thirteen, and several younger children. There is not a chair within the tumble-down apartment; the bedstead has a foul rug on it and no more clothing; in a corner under the sloping roof rustles some straw where the idiot boy lies. The old story—no work or prospect of it; no bread or prospect of it. The fire is almost out, and with it all light, all hope.

"We now arrive at a house where the staircase is so pitch dark that I have to grope my way up on my hands and knees. This is one of the cheerful abodes where forty-seven human beings are packed into six rooms. It is the strangest experience I have ever encountered. Here, in this hovel, children are about to

---

* *Daily Telegraph*, London, November 21, 1883.

be born ; here men and women are dying ; here new-born infants are yelling for food, guarded by baby nurses, whilst the expectant mother is off on some errand; here children of all ages and sizes swarm about the filthy floor with matted hair, and rags on their poor little bodies.

"We mount to the top of the house. We tap at the door, and it is opened. A picture-frame maker lives here, but he is out of work, as he needs must be since, in the first place, he has pawned his tools to get bread; and in the second, he has scarcely sufficient clothing to go out and search for employment. The wife is in bed, or rather she is rolled up on the floor in a filthy rug, for there is no bed, suffering from acute rheumatism. The fire is almost out, and one of the children, without any shoes or stockings, is hugging the cat that is kept to insure an absence of mice and rats for the sake of the wretched people compelled to lie on the floor. We hear no grumbling, no complaint, no execration, no despairing cry. Even these poor people with their empty stomachs and their fireless grates listen to a prayer when it is offered up though it sounds strangely under such circumstances. Talk to these people of the workhouse and they will refuse to discuss the question farther. The workhouse means separation from husband and child. They would rather starve or die here than that."

Such was the region in the midst of which an earnest man of God found himself stationed as a preacher of the Gospel. The ordinary means of grace were found to be here, as they are everywhere when faithfully and prayerfully used, efficient. Mr. Brown proved to be a popular preacher. Multitudes came to hear him, and scores and hundreds, through his words and the Spirit's power, were borne into the kingdom of God. But in a place like London, or indeed in any great city, large congregations may represent but small and limited sections of the people. So it was here : this great and flourishing church in all its religious work did not touch nor approach a very large portion of the community. Not one of the very poorest class,—of the people who stood most in need of the consolations of the Gospel,—would ever think of attending any of its regular or irregular services ; and those who did attend were a sifted and selected class composed of the most intelligent and well-to-do people of the community.

In the winter of 1879, when the length and severity of the season occasioned an unusual amount of distress, considerable sums of money were placed in the hands of Mr. Brown for the relief of the needy. The first plan adopted by him was that of distributing alms from his own home, but this soon proved impracticable. His door was continually besieged by throngs of applicants for aid, many of whom were quite unworthy of it, while the most deserving cases were the last to make their needs known. He accordingly employed two missionaries, both of them excellent men, and well fitted for their work, who went from house to house, through the most destitute streets, searching out the needy and supplying their wants in their own rooms. In this way he and his missionaries secured a welcome to about a thousand homes that had before been closed to Christ and Christian teachers. They thereupon resolved that "so open a door of usefulness should not be allowed to close." The matter was presented to the congregation and friends. They responded with liberal donations. The work which had been commenced as a temporary measure, to meet the exigencies of a severe winter, was accordingly established on a permanent basis and has been constantly expanding from that time to this.

It is assumed that when people are suffering the bitterness of extreme poverty their most pressing physical necessities must be relieved before their spiritual destitution can be successfully dealt with. It is also assumed that any system of relief work which aims at anything less or lower than the conversion of those for whom it labors to the Lord Jesus Christ, can give only a temporary and superficial sort of help. The plan is therefore adopted of first ministering to the immediate wants of the poor, feeding those who are found to be hungry and without food, clothing the tattered and half-naked, furnishing coal to the shivering and fireless, redeeming from pawn artisan's tools, garments and other necessities of life which famine has torn from them, providing medicines for the sick and helping the unemployed to find work. Secondly and simultaneously with their work for the relief of these physical necessities it is the custom of the missionaries then and there to preach the Gospel to the neglected people. Into the midst of the want, squalor, and sunless sadness of their wretched homes is brought the story of Christ's redeeming love ; the claims of God are personally urged ; salvation by the only Saviour is freely and affectionately offered; and these heathen in the heart of Christendom are taught to commit themselves with their wants to the fatherhood of God. "Our work," says Mr. Brown, "is seeking to save. This is carried

on amid the clean and squalid alike. There is no picking and choosing. Respectable or disreputable, they
need God's salvation. From room to room the missionaries make their way, sometimes discouraged, sometimes sickened, often saddened, but ever seeking by all
means to save some."

Nine missionaries, who give their whole time to such
work, were at last accounts employed by this church.
Not merely from house to house, but from room to
room they go, relieving the needy, visiting the sick,
consoling the afflicted, and preaching the Gospel everywhere. Their energetic leader declares that a missionary of experience never stops to talk in the entries,
never visits the lower rooms first, but goes to the very
top of a house to begin his work with its inmates and
"prays his way down," leaving no apartment unvisited,
where it is possible to gain admission. During the
year 1885, 26,340 visits were made by these missionaries. Those only are reckoned as visits where there
has been actual intercourse inside the people's rooms.
Relief in the shape of food was given in 8,428 in-
stances. The sick have been cared for to the number
of 3,938. During the year there were distributed upwards of 35,000 loaves of bread, 80 cwt. of rice, 35,000
lbs. of potatoes, and 1,000 lbs. of tea, besides 5,600
garments.

The missionaries, after spending most of the day in
visitation, hold evening meetings for the benefit of the
people among whom they have been working, in four
mission halls provided for the purpose. Each missionary has a regular personal and private interview with
the pastor once a week; and each sends in a weekly report, stating the kind and amount of relief given, the

number and locality of calls made, and the meetings held. Money is never given away except in very special cases. All relief is supplied by tickets, which are orders on the grocers and shop-keepers, or on a central office where tea and clothing are given out. As the tickets are given gradually in connection with the calls, there is never a rush upon the central office. All garments given away are stamped with Mr. Brown's name, and, therefore, cannot be accepted at the pawn-shops. The church and its friends also sustain an orphans' home and a seaside home for the exhausted and for convalescents, besides a great number of clubs, societies, meetings, and classes, such as have already been described.

The vigor and activity of the life enjoyed by the church is remarkable. No communion season passes— none has passed during the twenty years of the present pastorate—without accessions to its membership. On the occasion of our last visit, in July, 1886, we were informed that sixty persons were then waiting to be baptized within three weeks, which was said to be no extraordinary number. Most of these are not the fruits, or, at least, not the immediate fruits, of the mission work. It deals with persons so degraded that ordinary church services cannot affect them. They are lifted by degrees. They are first touched by the words of the missionary in their home, are then persuaded to visit the mission chapels, and are there lifted a step higher. They next learn to enjoy the prayer-meetings of the church, and are finally brought into the regular services of the Lord's house.

" Any week evening service," says the pastor, " there may be found at our tabernacle prayer-meeting those who used to lead drunken, abandoned, and, in some cases, indescribably vicious lives. We do not say that all these are truly converted, but to say the least, it is a glorious change from street-walking and public-house fighting. There is no hopeless class. Christ wins them all."

One naturally asks how any church, and especially one so largely composed of poor people, can possibly raise money enough to support such extensive missionary operations. In reply to this question, we quote again the correspondent of *The Daily Telegraph*:

"You ask me where the money comes from with which I am able to relieve these sorrows of Shadwell? Well, I am old-fashioned enough to believe in prayer. I pray for these wretched people night and day, and as yet I have never prayed in vain. Look here," and he led me to his study-table, where ever opened lies an ordinary ledger. "Glance at that last entry, if you please. 'A thank-offering for blessings given and many mercies vouchsafed, £75.' That is a donation; but I am to have the same sum every year, so long as my good friend lives. Please God, the ink-marks on that ledger will never long be dry."

The work is not advertised. No one but the Lord is ever asked for money or for help. Once a year the church appoints a day for receiving special thank-offerings, to be devoted to the mission work. A week-day is set apart as thank-offering day. Due notice having been given, the church is open from early morning, when men are going to their work, until late at night, and all day long the pastor is present to receive in person each gift from the hand of the giver. The offerings are of all sizes—poor workingmen bring a shilling or

two ; children contribute a few pence ; widows offer
their mite, and the few that are rich bring much. Each
donor, whether his gifts be small or great, is properly
credited with it in the books. As most of the people
are poor, the greater proportion of the money raised
comes in small sums of a few shillings each ; but taken
all together the thank-offerings usually amount to several hundred pounds. Besides this, donations for the
mission work pour in from all over England. Not a
farthing of debt is ever incurred ; yet means have never
been lacking for the continuance and expansion of the
work.

Christian workers in London have experienced the
same difficulty in retaining their influence over the
older boys of the Sunday-school that has perplexed so
many of us here. Our attention was directed to one
very interesting and successful effort to overcome this
difficulty, which is well worthy of study.

The Regent Square Presbyterian Church, of which
Dr. Oswald Dykes is pastor, had a flourishing mission,
since then become a church, in Somerstown, a poor
neighborhood in Northwest London. Connected with
this mission was a large Sunday-school, composed almost entirely of artisans' children. Great numbers of
small children and of larger girls attended the school ;
but the boys, after reaching the age of fourteen or fifteen, became possessed of the notion that they were too
big for Sunday-school, and so left it, and were soon
estranged from religious influences of all kinds, so that
the work done for the boys' classes seemed like water
poured on the ground. For the sake of saving these
lads, after much thought and prayer, *an institute for
working lads* was planned and organized. It commenced

very modestly, with a small membership, and provided at first only a small room for reading and club room, a Bible-class, and one or two evening classes. But it grew and extended its operations rapidly. Commodious quarters in an old chapel were secured; a gymnasium, a library and reading-room, and evening classes were successively added; games were provided, a regular ground for cricket and football was hired; meetings and entertainments of all sorts were held, and now the "top story of the Sunday-school," as the *Aldenham Institute* is sometimes called, is wonderfully popular. It has a membership of over four hundred, and the average small boy of that Sunday-school has no higher ambition than to become a member of it, a thing not allowed until he has reached the age of fifteen.

There are three Bible-classes in the week. A guild with daily Bible-readings and monthly meetings comprises a large portion of its members. They have a course of "ambulance instruction" on first aid to the injured, art classes, classes in English literature and composition, in English grammar and elocution, in political economy, singing, writing, arithmetic, bookkeeping, French, German, and nine different science classes, besides technical instruction in carpentry, plumbers' work, printing, and lithography.

As most of the members are young, and all of them engaged in tedious toil during the day, the Institute performs no slight service in providing them with healthy play. It has a chess and draughts (checkers) club, a cricket club, a football club, a swimming club, and a club of "harriers," for the old-fashioned English game of hare-and-hounds.

The Institute has, in many ways, been of almost

priceless value to its members. By taking up the evenings and holidays which most boys of that class simply idle away on the streets or in worse places, and filling them with helpful instruction and healthful amusement, it has lifted its members quite out of the old degraded life to which they were born and seemed to be doomed. When the president, a warm-hearted British merchant, had conducted the writer through two or three rooms full of the young fellows engaged in their usual employments, the latter exclaimed: " Why, these are not working lads! " " No," was the reply, " it is true that they are nearly all clerks; but working lads they all have been, and working lads they still would be were it not for this Institute."

In speaking within so limited a space upon so great a theme as that of Christian work in London, it has been necessary to select a very few characteristic items for presentation out of the vast amount of material at hand, and it has seemed wisest to dwell on those forms of work that are more or less directly connected with local churches. But it should not be forgotten that a very large proportion of the religious effort in that city, especially that which deals with the needs of the poor, has no connection with any local church. There are multitudes of independent missions of all sorts, many of them well worth studying, of which we can make no mention. It will not do, however, to pass by without a word of notice the most remarkable of them all, namely: *The London City Mission.** This great organization has, for fifty years, been carrying the Gospel silently, but with exceeding power, into the dark and cruel

---

* See *These Fifty Years*, John Matthias Weyland. London, 1884.

places of the great town. It works in the interest of no denomination—is supported by collections made from all the churches and by donations from Christians of every name and order. Its missionaries, of whom there are now about five hundred, are chiefly occupied in carrying the Gospel from house to house in the neglected parts of the city, in distributing tracts and portions of the Scriptures, and in ministering to the sick and dying. Upwards of three millions of such calls were reported last year, of which two hundred and seventy thousand were calls upon the sick. Besides this general work the society has appointed a large number of special missionaries for the benefit of certain classes whose peculiar circumstances have shut them out from the regular means of grace. Missionaries are employed by the society who give their whole time to work for policemen, for bakers, for night and day cabmen, for drovers, for omnibus and tram-carmen, for soldiers and sailors, for fire brigades, for theatre employés, for hotel servants, for canalboat men, for coachmen and grooms, for letter-carriers and telegraph boys, for railway-men and navvies, for gypsies, for fallen women, and for thieves. A score or so of missionaries are exclusively engaged in visiting public-houses, gin-palaces, and coffee-shops. The missionaries also conduct a great number of Bible-readings and evangelistic meetings, some of which are held in workhouses, penitentiaries, hospitals, and factories, and many in the open air.

Street meetings are very common in London. You will hear the voice of prayer, Gospel melodies, and earnest preaching by the wayside in scores of places all over the great city on any pleasant Sunday afternoon or during the long twilight of the summer evenings. The parks are the favorite places, however, for open-air services. On every Sunday afternoon several such meetings are carried on at the same time and side by side both in Regent's Park and Hyde Park. Besides half a dozen meetings for preaching the Gospel, one of which is always conducted in the German language, there are usually two or three for the proclamation of Socialism, and others in which the credibility of the Christian religion is discussed in alternate attacks made by some representative of infidelity and defences by some Christian. London has a *Society of Christian Evidences*, which gives particular attention to training young men for work of this sort. Many churches in poorer neighborhoods preface their evening services by brief open-air meetings. The value of such preaching may be questioned. It shocks one's sensibilities, at first, to hear sacred things cried out amid the shifting, laughing, trifling crowd out for a holiday. Yet the careful observer will rarely fail to find one or two real listeners at every such meeting. We know of one large and flourishing church situated in a neighborhood of great poverty and vice which sprang out of an open-air movement combined with a mission Sunday-school in the first place, and, having continued its out-of-door services until the present time, has actually gathered a large portion of its members from the streets.

A discussion of Christian work among the masses of London would be incomplete without some reference to that singular religious movement called *The Salvation Army*. The nature and methods of this organiza tion are too well known to require description ; but in order to be intelligently understood they should be studied on their native soil. About twenty years ago, when there was far less religious and philanthropic work for the poor than now, a certain unknown Wesleyan minister, William Booth by name, touched by the misery and godlessness of the place, commenced preaching the Gospel to the poor on a waste piece of land near Mile End Road, East London. Out of that humble beginning sprang the Salvation Army at whose head Mr. Booth continues to stand, the "General" of a host whose officers are now numbered by thousands and the soldiers by hundreds of thousands, and whose operations are extended around the globe.

This is a mission from the lower classes, by the lower classes, and for the lower classes. It speaks to the common people in their own manner and their native language. The vernacular of the slums of London is practically a different language from that of the prayer-book and the pulpit. Religion, as the Church ordinarily teaches it, is presented in a tongue half unknown to the day laborer. The missionaries to the Indians have best succeeded in converting them, not by teaching them English first and then presenting the Gospel in English, but by translating the truth into their own rough speech and bringing its messages home to their heart on the wings of the mother-tongue; so it is the plan of the Salvation Army to translate the messages of salvation into the rude lingo of the dock-yard and the gin-palace in order that it may reach those who know no other language. For the same reason its music and its religious meetings resemble the entertainments given in cheap theatres and low concert halls.

It has many excellent features. The earnestness and courage of its leaders and their enthusiasm for the salvation of the very lowest cannot be too highly praised. The plainness of its speech and the faithfulness and power with which it bears its testimony are to be commended. Much of the criticism urged against it is unjust. Utterances of its members that seem shockingly irreverent and actions that seem rude, take that appearance because the observer judges from his own point of view and is unable to appreciate the sincerity from which they spring. It is, however, undoubtedly the case that the Salvation Army furnishes a striking illustration of the truth that the religion of a class, whether the class be high or low, must always be a narrow and one-sided religion. This movement, being exclusively one of the lower classes, lacks just those elements that the presence of cultured members would give it. It needs ballast. It is enthusiastic, couragous, and hearty; but it is neither wise, nor thorough, nor profound. There is an excessive amount of evangelistic appeal ; there is a grievous lack of religious and Biblical instruction. As to the value of its work on the whole, it is not easy to speak with certainty. We have found a great variety of opinions regarding it. Of its value in one direction, however, there is but one opinion. It has had a great influence in stirring up the churches to an appreciation of the needs of the poor and their duty toward the outcast.

It is encouraging to believe that the religious work of London is not without effect. There has been progress in the condition of the working-classes within twenty-five years. Slowly, but surely, headway is making against the awful current of sin and misery. There is less drunkenness, less pauperism, and less crime in the great metropolis to-day than ten years ago. The missionary spirit is abroad in the churches and increases from year to year. "With God all things are possible,"—and it is one of the modern miracles to see a city growing better while she daily adds to her immensity.

CHAPTER VI.

THE McALL MISSION.

In our day God has raised up one man and sent him with signs and wonders to be an apostle to the perishing masses of a great and godless city.

Rev. Robert W. McAll, the pastor of an English Congregational church, crossed the Channel with Mrs. McAll for the first time in the summer of 1871 to spend a short vacation on the Continent. Four days of this visit were allotted to Paris. That city had just been passing through the dreadful experience with which the Franco-Prussian war came to its close. The smoke of the besieging cannon had scarcely cleared away, fresh wounds were still bleeding, the horrors of famine had but just subsided, and the wretched poor in their want and misery were utterly destitute of the consolations of religion. Prompted by a yearning of heart over the unfortunate people, Mr. and Mrs. McAll resolved to spend their last evening at Paris in distributing tracts and Scripture portions. Notwithstanding the protests of friends, they went alone to that miserable quarter named Belleville, whose gloomy houses in days of trouble know how to pour out troops of gaunt, hungry men and furious women to swell the Commune. They took their stand under the gas that blazes in front of a great wine-vault on the corner of Rue de Belleville and the Boulevard, and they commenced to offer tracts to the thronging passers-by.

A crowd of poor people gathered about them in no time, eager to receive the little gifts; and at length one in a workingman's blouse stood forth from among his fellows and said in English: "Sir, are you not an English minister? If so, I have something of importance to say to you. You are at this moment in the very midst of a district inhabited by thousands and tens of thousands of us, workingmen To a man we have done with an imposed religion, a religion of superstition and oppression. But if any one would come to teach us religion of another kind—a religion of freedom and earnestness—many of us are ready to listen." *

In that pleading face, seen for but one brief moment, yet never to be forgotten, McAll beheld his "Man of Macedonia."

He had already passed the "dead-line" of fifty. He was wholly ignorant of the French language He had never even visited Paris before, and was utterly unacquainted with its people and its ways. His kindred and friends and all his interests were in England. As pastor of an important church at Hadley which had two missions of its own, his sphere of usefulness at home was by no means insignificant. If any one could be excused from a foreign mission he was that man— so urged his friends. But he saw the matter differently. There were men enough ready to fill his place at Hadley. He had sufficient income for a modest support without a salary. The fields of France were

---

* *A Cry from the Land of Calvin and Voltaire.* Records of the McAll Mission, p. 9, London, 1887.

"white already to harvest," and there were no reapers. He felt that he must go.

Five months later Mr. and Mrs. McAll again walked together amid the crowds of Rue de Belleville. This time they were not distributing tracts, but invitations to their first meeting, which was held in a small shop fitted up as a mission hall. They had chosen a home in the neighborhood and were resolved to give the rest of their lives to the work of the Gospel among the common people of Paris. McAll had only two sentences of French with which to begin the great crusade, —"God loves you," and "I love you." But when men saw that those two were messages which came from a sincere and fervent heart, they believed them and received them gladly. Twenty-eight persons attended the first meeting. Within the fifteen years that have elapsed since then, the single mission hall has become one hundred, thirty-four of them situated in Paris and environs, in which nearly seventeen thousand meetings have been held and more than a million persons gathered for religious instruction in the course of the past year.

The city to which this modern apostle was sent with his message of life was one of peculiar spiritual destitution. The grasp of the Roman .Church upon the French, especially upon Parisians, became feebler with every year. She had lost the respect and confidence of the common people, and had consequently, to a' great extent, forfeited her influence over them. They suspected her of hostility to free institutions and popular education. They resented her assumption of the right to interpose her authority in secular affairs. Her priests were esteemed to be lovers of money rather than lovers of men, and flatterers of the rich instead of friends to the poor. The inconsistency of many of her teachings and claims with reason and sound common sense was keenly felt. She had in large measure ceased to bear the water of life to the thirsting people; her fountain was dried up and full of dust; her cup was empty. Multitudes turned away from her in disgust to rationalism,—to animalism,—to thoughtless, hopeless unbelief.

The Protestants of France, meanwhile, were able to do, or at all events were doing little to save those whom the emptiness of Rome had driven into irreligion. Although the churches of the Huguenots had never been quite extinguished, and had been tolerated and even supported by the State since the time of the first Napoleon, they had lived as it were in a strait-jacket. They had been hampered by numerous restrictions and petty persecutions urged on under legal sanction by their enemies. Until within a few years Protestants had no legal right to burial in ground set apart for the sacred rest of the dead, but found a place there only on sufferance. "They might not hold the stated services of their religion except with government permission and under government surveillance, which not only fixed days and hours and place of meeting, but had a right to intervene in the matter of the doctrine taught. All special or irregular meetings, as for prayer or conference, were prohibited, except under special sanction; and failing that, could only be safely convened by means of formal invitations to a private house, issued as for a private social gathering. To distribute religious notices, handbills, tracts, or other printed matter, without a colporteur's license, was equally illegal. The printed invitations to the McAll meetings were all thus illegally distributed up to 1878 and during the earlier years, before the work had come to be thoroughly appreciated, never without a certain degree of risk. Two of the young ladies of the Mission were, indeed, arrested in 1873 for distributing printed announcements of a meeting, although that very meeting had been authorized by the Prefect of the Police. The young ladies were released without difficulty. At that time, and for several years later, it was contrary to law to make proselytes or to give Protestant instruction to the children of non-Protestants. All the missionary and evangelizing agencies of the Protestant churches were carried on under laws which permitted merely the instructing anew, and confirming in the faith of nominal Protestants—those who were such by baptism or inheritance." *

" It was not so very long before this time that a missionary of the London Bible Society had been tried in the French courts for offering a room in his house for religious meetings and for *swindling ;* that is, for taking up voluntary contributions for religious purposes. On the first count he was condemned, fined, and imprisoned for two months, and though not condemned on the second count, he was severely reprimanded by the judge, who said that such a proceeding was virtually swindling under the law, and would so be treated if it occurred again " †

Such repression of evangelistic effort was unfavor-

---

* *French Protestantism in the Nineteenth Century.* By Louise Seymour Houghton, pp. 4 and 5. Published by the American McAll Association. Philadelphia, 1886.

† Ibid., p. 6.

able to the spiritual health of the Protestant churches. Rationalism became wide-spread among them, and did its part in quenching religious zeal. Thus, hampered without and weakened within, being, moreover, few in number, poor and uninfluential, the Reformed churches of fifteen years ago were doing little more than to care for those of their own household. The common people of Paris, and other cities as well, repelled in vast numbers from the Roman Catholic Church, and not won by the Protestants, were therefore left in woful ignorance of all religious truth.

The great preachers and revivalists of England and America have usually addressed themselves and adapted their measures to the needs of a people who were already somewhat familiar with the fundamental facts of our faith. Such methods of conducting evangelistic meetings and doing Christian work as commonly prevail among us, therefore assume that those with whom they deal accept the Bible as the word of God, and know something of its cardinal doctrines. But for the masses of Paris,—for a people to whom no other light had come than such distorted and discolored rays as could penetrate the deep-stained windows of Catholicism,—the ordinary religious methods of England and America were found to be in many respects inadequate and unsuitable.

Mr. McAll declares that there are "hundreds of thousands in Paris itself who, up to this day, have literally never had a Bible in their hands, nor have come once within the sound of the preaching of justification by faith." * The following account of the ex-

---

* *A Cry from the Land of Calvin and Voltaire*, p. 23.

perience of an intelligent man, a landed proprietor who was in the habit of spending six months of every year in Paris, is scarcely credible, and vividly illustrates what McAll has termed "the prevailing *oblivion* of the Book in France." This man having been persuaded to attend one of the meetings, said to the leader at its close, "What book is that you read from, sir?" "The Bible! or what we call 'La Parole de Dieu.'" "The Bible! Could you lend it me for a week? I will bring it back. I never heard these words before!" "Oh," replied the preacher, "I will give you a Gospel," and handed him the Gospel of John. He thanked him, gave his card, and went away. Next Tuesday he returned the Gospel, saying, "That is not the book you read from; cannot you lend me ⟁HE BOOK?" "Certainly," was the answer; so I gave him a copy. It was small, and he found out where to buy one, and went and bought a large Bible for himself. "Strange," he said, "I never saw this book before, and since hearing you read it I went to three booksellers in Batignolles, intending to buy it; but they could neither supply it nor tell me where to procure one. Then I sent my wife, hoping she might succeed, and she came back with this statement, 'It was a bad book, a forbidden book, and only used by priests and pastors.' So I was afraid I could not get it. Now I shall read it, measure and weigh every word." *

Another characteristic of the people whom the McAll Mission seeks to save, is an astonishing ignorance of the fact and nature of sin. Speaking of this matter, Mr. McAll remarks: "We would not conceal the im-

---

* *A Cry from the Land of Calvin and Voltaire*, p. 46.

mense obstacles to Gospel-prevalence which the actual
state of the masses of the French people interposes.
We dare not say that conscience is tender; far otherwise, alas! A vast work remains to be effected in the
awakening of the inward monitor. The entire tendency
of Romish practices and teachings through a succession of centuries has been to lull conscience into a deep
sleep. True insight of sin, as heart-rebellion against
our heavenly Father, is rare indeed. . . . . Throughout fifteen years' history of our work we have been
constantly meeting with surprising examples of the
prevailing inaction, the *deadness* of conscience." * A
young man said to a missionary, "I admire and delight
in the meetings, but you are always talking to sinners.
For my part, I am no sinner. I have nothing with
which to reproach myself. I have never wronged any
one." " No, I have never sinned," said a woman indig-
nantly. "To be sure," she added, "I have sometimes
said my fish was fresh when it wasn't ; but then God
knew that was for my interest, and He will not blame
me."

Furthermore, such notions of religious matters as do
prevail are distorted and even fantastic. This is well illustrated by a story from one of the children's meetings:

" The lesson for the day chanced to be on prayer and
the gift of the Holy Spirit. The speaker . . . . pro-
ceeded to explain to the children what was meant by
praying for spiritual graces, using language and illustrations so thoroughly level with their intellectual
capacities, that the greatest quiet reigned in the *salle*,
and intelligence seemed to beam on every face. The

---

* *A Cry from the Land of Calvin and Voltaire*, pp. 24 and 25.

teacher, greatly encouraged, finished by saying, 'Now, how many of you have already prayed for spiritual graces?' Up went several hands, but on investigation most of these morning devotions resolved themselves into repetitions, more or less exact, of the Lord's Prayer. One boy, however, the model boy of the school, persisted in his assertion that to the 'Notre Père' he had added something which answered to his teacher's description of a prayer for spiritual graces." After some persuasion he repeated, in all soberness and good faith, as an example of a prayer for spiritual grace, a few verses, of which the following is a literal translation. It is said that they may be found in many Catholic books of devotion :

"As the Holy Virgin was walking through the fields, on her way she met St. John.

"'St. John, whence come you?'

"'I have just been saying my prayers.'

"'Have you seen my Child Jesus?'

"'Yes, dear lady, I saw Him on the Cross, with nails in His hands, His side pierced, and on His head a crown of white thorns.'

"Those who repeat this prayer morning and night will never see the flames of hell." *

In seeking to meet the needs of such a people Mr. McAll was led to the discovery and adoption of a system of city evangelization which is in certain important respects peculiar to himself—a system whose phenomenal success proves its value. Now the religious condition of the working-class, who compose so large a proportion of the population of modern American

---

* *A Cry from the Land of Calvin and Voltaire*, pp. 169 and 170.

cities, does not differ so widely as one may suppose
from that of the same class in Paris. Most of them
have come, they or their parents, from the Continent of
Europe, or from Catholic Ireland, and sixty per cent.
of these are of Roman Catholic stock. As we have
observed, the American Protestant churches have thus
far succeeded in getting hold of but a very small proportion of them. The Roman Church has probably
succeeded better in maintaining its influence among its
followers here than in France; yet it is certain that vast
numbers of its people, and perhaps even greater numbers of nominal Protestants, have been slipping away
from the churches of their fathers into irreligion and
unbelief. It will hardly be questioned that the workingmen of our towns and cities, in their religious condition, far more closely resemble the multitudes who
are gathered into the *salles* of the McAll Mission than
those who have composed the audiences of such men
as Wesley, Whitfield, Nettleton, Kirk, Finney, or even
Spurgeon and Moody. A study of the methods employed in this remarkable movement ought therefore
to be of value to all who are interested in that problem
which stands among the foremost of our age, the religious problem of American cities.

The first to be noted and the most remarkable among
the peculiarities of method adopted by the McAll Mission, regards the character of the *Salles*, or Mission Halls,
in which the meetings are held. Ordinary shops front-
ing on frequented streets are usually rented and fitted up
for this purpose. The halls are thus always comparatively small. The largest in Paris has sittings for only
450 persons; four or five others accommodate as many
as 300 each; the rest seat from 80 to 260 each. Great

advantages are claimed for this system. In the first place, such rooms are always easily secured in any part of the city where they are needed. Large halls, intended for auditoriums, are not easy to find—are not likely to be located where the Mission wants them, and are hard to get the entire control of ; but there are always and everywhere shops to be had at a reasonable rent. The ground floors of most of the buildings in Paris are arranged for shops. This system also has the advantage of being much less expensive than the ordinary plan. Large halls cannot be leased so as to be used exclusively for mission purposes, without considerable expense; it is still more costly to secure property and erect chapels or other buildings in the crowded districts where missions are most needed, but the rent of ordinary shops is much more easily managed. This is an important matter. One of the greatest difficulties in all benevolent and mission work arises from lack of funds. The field is always opening faster than it can be supplied with men and money. Owing to the high rents and expensive living, mission work in great cities is especially costly It is one of the marvels of the McAll Mission that so much has been accomplished at so small an expense. The whole cost of maintaining the ninety-nine mission halls, thirty-four of them in and about the costly city of Paris, during the year 1886, including rents, salaries, new furniture, taxes, cost of administration, and every expense of every sort, was less than $80,000. There are single institutions in England and America whose annual expenditure is much greater.

It is furthermore claimed in favor of the small meetings that they are much more easily equipped with

speakers than great ones. A large audience can only
be effectively addressed by a man of extraordinary
power. Such men are rare and their services always
difficult to secure. But a man of smaller calibre can do
equally good work in a smaller meeting. Other things
being equal, many little meetings are more useful than
a few large ones In the former the speaker is brought
into closer contact with the hearer, his influence is
more forcible, his message more personal, and each
auditor involuntarily takes a larger share of it to himself. In a small meeting it is also possible, as it never
is in the case of a great assembly, to extend a cordial
welcome to every one who enters, to observe the effect
of the discourse upon all, and to follow up the preaching
by personal effort.

Shops have still another advantage over chapels and
large halls for mission purposes : they are much more
accessible to the throngs of the street. Made so as to
be easily entered, but a single step from the sidewalk,
they open their inviting doors to those who, fatigued
with walking, desire a few moments' rest; to those who
are prompted by curiosity to enter, and to all who for
any reason care to go in. An illumination, suspended
over the sidewalk before the door, announces, in blaz-
ing letters, the name and character of the hall and the
time of the meetings, and extends to all a cordial invitation to attend them.

Another peculiarity of the McAll system is seen in
the careful appointment of an *outer* and an *inner doorkeeper* for every meeting. The former service is performed by a gentleman who stands on the sidewalk in
front of the entrance and distributes printed invitations
to the passers-by, enforcing their message as often as

possible by a kind word of welcome. Those who enter are received by the inner doorkeeper, a lady, who politely welcomes each one as a guest, shows him a seat and provides him with a hymn-book. This lady— in the larger halls there are two of them—" is charged with the multifarious offices of inner gatekeeper, deputy hostess, hall policeman and superior, tract and New Testament distributer, general informant, and, later on, friend and visitor to those who accept the invitation handed them at the door and enter." Great pains are taken in filling these two appointments. Neither place is ever allowed to be vacant for a single meeting, and they are never occupied by servants or paid employés of the Mission, nor by people of the working-class, but by ladies and gentlemen who love the cause of Christ. It is held that the invitation of a gentleman is much more likely to be favorably received by the average Parisian than that of a commoner, and that the gracious welcome of a lady is peculiarly pleasing. The lady doorkeepers are, moreover, found to be remarkably successful in maintaining order in the meetings. Whenever some rough fellow shows symptoms of becoming turbulent, a simple request from a lady is usually enough to subdue him. It touches the hearts of the poor to have those who are so greatly their superiors in wealth and station come to them as friends and helpers. The English and American residents of Paris have served largely in this capacity.

The halls within are neatly but plainly furnished, so that the humblest auditors, while attracted by their cheerfulness, may not be oppressed by unfamiliar elegance.

A service of song, conducted by a lady who presides at the cabinet organ, invariably opens the meeting.

The music of the Gospel has had marvellous power—has given wings to the truth in Paris. France is said to be poor in song. She has the heavy, classic music of the cathedral, she has the opera, but there are few pure, simple songs for the people, either religious or secular. One of the most important services rendered by the McAll Mission to the French people has, therefore, been the collection, translation, and introduction of Christian hymns. Mrs. McAll has done most of this work. The three hundred and more hymns that are now in use in the Mission include both popular "Gospel Songs," such as, "Hold the Fort" and "I love to tell the Story," and at the same time many of the choicest lyrics of the church.

After the song-service, which is greatly enjoyed, a passage of Scripture is read, and the meeting is then addressed in turn by two speakers. The addresses are short, not exceeding fifteen minutes each, and a hymn comes between them. All polemics are, by an inflexible rule, forbidden. Not one word derogatory to the Roman Catholic Church, or even to rationalism, must be spoken. The addresses are not to be learned, rhetorical, or philosophical; their single aim must be to present simply, clearly, vividly, and positively the great facts of our faith. The single, brief prayer of the evening follows the second address, and then, after the concluding hymn, the audience is dismissed, not with a benediction, but with a simple "Good-night," and a cordial invitation to come again. As the people go out, the workers have an opportunity to speak with any who seem especially interested, to hand them tracts or portions of the Scriptures, and to get their addresses in order to call upon them on the following day.

The appointments for all the meetings are made with consummate skill from the central office. At least five persons must serve at every meeting that is held—the gentleman outside the door, the lady within, the organist, and the two speakers. Each of these persons must accept his appointment, and a card from him must be received on which he agrees to be present at the specified time and place. As over eighty meetings of this kind for adults, besides half as many more Sunday-schools, mothers' meetings, etc., must be provided for regularly every week, in Paris and its suburbs alone, it will readily be seen that the task of administration is no simple one; yet so skillfully is it performed that the whole system moves on with perfect smoothness, and it rarely happens that a single position is left unfilled.

Nearly all the speakers are volunteers. They place themselves at the disposal of the Mission for a certain number of evenings each week or month, as the case may be, and are sent out wherever they are required. It is a labor of love, and they receive no pay beyond their carriage fare. About fifty pastors and one hundred and fifty laymen have given more or less of their time to such work in Paris during the past year. Great pains are taken to select for each field the speakers best adapted to its need. It is usually so arranged that one of the two speakers appointed for a place is decidedly stronger than the other. The second of the two addresses is assigned to him, and he is given charge of the meeting The doorkeepers usually remain at the same hall night after night, but the speakers are changed about from place to place

In several of the more important halls meetings are held every evening of the week at 8 or 8:15 o'clock.

12

Most of the others have two, three, or four meetings in the course of the week. A Sunday-school is held in nearly all of them on Sunday afternoon, and a children's meeting in the middle of the week. During eight months of the year working-meetings for women, similar to the mothers' meetings of England, are held every week in fifteen of the different halls. Besides these there are numerous prayer - meetings, Bible-classes, young men's and young women's meetings, Bible union meetings, fraternal society meeting, etc., etc.

The converts of the mission are, so far as possible, persuaded to join the regular Protestant churches of the city, of which there are forty, "where the Gospel is preached in simplicity and in sincerity." * There are, however, many in whom the prejudice against the name "Protestant," and against everything churchly is so deeply rooted that they cannot be prevailed upon to take this step. Such persons are banded together in what are termed *Sociétés Fraternelles*. The following are the rules of one of these societies :

1. " Every member must believe on the Lord Jesus Christ.

2. " Every member engages to read every day a portion of Scripture.

3. " Every member engages to pray for his associates, and to visit them in time of sickness.

4. " Every member engages to pay a monthly contribution of at least one penny on behalf of the poor."

"It meets every fortnight for prayer, edification, and

---

* See *Yesterday and To-day ; or, The Activities of French Protestants.* A pamphlet by Westphal Castelman, with Introduction by Rev. A. F. Beard, D.D. Paris, 1885.

testimony. New members are admitted after two
months' probation as candidates ; absence unaccounted
for during three months, or conduct contrary to the
morals of the Gospel, are causes of erasure." It is intended by means of these organizations, not only to
keep together, to instruct, and to train young believers,
but to give them more intelligent notions of the nature
of the Christian Church and their obligation to become
its members.

Contributions have never been asked for at the regular evangelistic meetings. The conduct of the Church
of Rome in France has been such as to give currency
to the opinion that religion is simply a money-making
matter. The freedom of the Gospel presented by the
McAll Mission has been one of its strongest attractions.
" How much to pay ? " is often a stranger's first question as he enters a hall. When offered a seat, he asks
again, " What does it cost ? " And when a hymn-book
is handed to him, he still expects to be charged for it.
The idea that pure, disinterested love has invited him
to come in and seeks his benefit, is one that he grasps
slowly and with astonishment, but when he has grasped
it, it moves him powerfully.

From the nature of the case, and from the character
of the methods employed, it is impossible to give in
figures any approximate notion of the results accomplished by the McAll Mission. We only know that the
Gospel is being preached in purity and fervor to audiences whose aggregate number is more than a million
a year, and that multitudes of these are converted to
the truth. How many, we have no means of telling.
The converts are not counted, nor are they kept together as members of any one organization. As fast

as men are led to Christ they are handed over to the
regular Protestant churches. The mission aims to be
the ally, the feeder of the churches. It lives not for
itself, but for them. The value of its services to French
Protestantism and to the French people has been finely
stated by one who speaks from an intimate acquaintance with the whole subject, the Rev. A. F. Beard, D D.,
former pastor of the American Church in Paris. In
his words we shall close this chapter :

"It is to the credit of the Mission McAll that it forms
no churches. It could perhaps introduce one more sect
in France, and perhaps plant a little ' ism.' But it does
not need to do this, and the broad-minded and clear-
eyed man who gave this Mission its stamp belongs to
Christianity.

"It is hoped that the existing Protestant churches
will reap rich harvests from this Mission. They have
already the first-fruits. But aside from this, there is a
relation of the McAll Mission to the churches which is
very important. It has brought to the churches of
France the inspiration of Christian aggressiveness, and
the examples and illustrations of simple and successful
methods. It is not speaking unkindly of the French
churches to say that from the very necessities of past
condition they had much to learn, both as to the spirit
of aggressive Christian work and the methods of it.
They had lived a repressed life. They had been forbidden by law to evangelize. They had come, in the
nature of the case, to a dignified and somewhat formal
style of worship. The services were ' churchly.'

"The McAll Mission has been a constant ' object-
lesson,' illustrating how the Gospel may be earnestly
preached in a popular way. It has given examples of

Christian work in its various phases; it has shown even in the most difficult quarters that the people can be reached. That which Protestant pastors thought could not be done, has been done, and this has been a great awakening power of Christian aggression, both as to spirit and method. The conservative instincts of many good men have yielded to the influence.

"Barriers between the unchurched and the churched have been taken down, and those who knew nothing of church life, except to distrust it, and who had an untruthful idea of Christianity, have been made to feel that pastors are not unsympathetic persons who preach from a high pulpit of propriety to those who can pay for it, but are indeed their friends, true, earnest hearts who love them as souls; and that their words are not official commonplaces expected to be uttered, but utterances revealing hearts full of sympathy for man as man. If the McAll Mission had done no more than to *come close to the people*, and to those most needy, as an object-lesson to churches which have been the subject of repression and persecution, it would have justified its life. It becomes incidentally also a grand training-school for the future evangelism of France in its direct, simple, and sincere presentation of the Gospel. It meets the questions of the Papacy and of Infidelity not controversially, but by constant insistance of Gospel truths, so that thousands listen with sympathy whom controversy could never reach." *

---

* *Yesterday and To-day*, Introduction, pp. 11-13.

CHAPTER VII.

In our first three chapters attention has been called to the fact that the population of the United States has, for the past hundred years, been shifting with great rapidity from the rural parts into the towns. We have seen that the causes to which this change is due are still operative, and seem likely to remain so for many years; so that the cities of to-day, great as they appear, are small in comparison with what they will probably become. We have seen that their increase in size is accompanied by growing class distinctions; that the so-called "working-people," who compose the majority of the population of modern towns, are separated from others, not only by many such differences in birth, education, occupation, and estate as divide the social classes of Europe, but by additional barriers of difference in race, language, and religion. We have seen that in consequence of these differences, the American Protestant churches, upon whose high faith and its outcome in pure morality our civilization stands, have largely failed to reach the working-classes in the towns and have become too much the churches of the well-to-do, while the poor have been left to Catholicism, to irreligion, and to infidelity; and we have seen that the irreligion of these masses who chiefly people the cities has been naturally followed by a decay of morality in the cities, and by such alarming symptoms of the disintegration of Christian civilization as a rapid increase of crime, of pauperism, of intemperance, and Sabbath desecration, and a growing spirit of anarchy among workingmen In the fourth and fifth chapters we examined, as far as possible in so brief a space, the methods of religious work which prevail in London, and in the sixth those of the McAll Mission in Paris, hoping to receive from beyond the Atlantic some hints that may be helpful in the solution of our own difficult problems The closing chapter will be devoted to a few suggestions concerning Christian work for our cities which are made in view of the gravity of the situation here, and in the light of such wisdom as we have culled from abroad.

We remark, in the first place, that it seems tolerably certain, if the churches hope to reach the people, that they must greatly enlarge their working force in the towns and cities. The greatest of our troubles is, that far too little whole-hearted, thorough-going, thoughtful endeavor is put forth for the salvation of the poorer classes. "The harvest truly is plenteous, but the laborers are few" No more striking difference appears between the ways of our English brethren and our own, than the difference in the number of regular paid workers employed by an ordinary church in the two countries. Over against their corps of clergymen, missionaries, Bible readers, deaconesses, and trained nurses, stands our pastor, single - handed, or, in exceptional cases, with one or two assistants. Is it a wonder that they accomplish a vast deal more than we?

Most American ministers are obliged to depend for assistance entirely upon the voluntary aid of laymen.

Now, although such aid is of great importance, and can never be dispensed with, it is too fitful and irregular to be reliable except when well organized and closely superintended. The pastor has no more difficult task than that of keeping his people engaged in efficient, systematic Christian work. If the increase of the regular force of the church were likely, by taking the responsibility off from the shoulders of private members, to diminish the amount of voluntary service, it would not be an unmixed good; but we are confident that the opposite result would follow such an increase. As a general can get more fighting out of his soldiers when assisted by a staff of subordinate officers than if he attempted the command alone, so a pastor can best succeed in supplying work for every willing heart in the congregation when assisted in carrying out his plans by suitable helpers. Recent observation in England confirms this belief. Notwithstanding the number of paid workers, the rank and file of the people appear, to say the least, quite as deeply engaged in Christian service there as here.

But there are certain branches of parochial work that cannot well be delegated to volunteers. In a large parish, duties of this kind are often enough, of themselves alone, when done as well as they should be, to absorb more than the entire strength of one, or even two pastors. The larger the proportion of poor and humble people in the parish, the greater is its need of thorough and laborious parish work. With all classes, personal, hand-to-hand presentation of the truth is doubtless worthy of far stronger emphasis than it has usually received; but this is especially the case with the lowly. The best results cannot be secured among such people unless pulpit instruction is both prepared for and supplemented by abundant personal work. It is, therefore, frequently the case that the pastor of a church in a large parish has three or four times as much depending upon him alone as he can possibly perform. He is obliged to do what he can and let the rest go. This is a wasteful method. On the one hand, there is not enough parish work done to make the preaching properly effective, and, on the other hand, too much parish work is done to leave sufficient time for the preparation of sermons. It is not businesslike; it is not the way careful men proceed in other matters. Look at the Roman Catholics. How thoroughly well they man every point they take. Small indeed is the church of that communion which employs a single, unassisted priest. Their great city churches where thousands of working-people resort on every Sabbath, are often served by half a score of priests. Does not their remarkable success in winning the poor and retaining their influence over the lowly, both here and in all other lands, suggest that there may be something in their methods worth our study ?

A minister's assistants need not, however, be fully educated and equipped clergymen. One man, if he has his time, can do preaching enough for a whole church however large. In a poor parish, an uneducated person, full of the Holy Ghost, may be a much more efficient helper than a college graduate. It is a fact which experience has demonstrated over and over again, both here, in England, and in heathen lands, that the best workers among any class are those who have come up from among that class. If you wish to reach the patrons of the saloons, send them one whom the grace of God has saved from drunkenness, and however much his uncouth language and his apparent irreverence may shock the wise and prudent, he will win men that the polished clergyman could not touch with the tip of his fingers.

A London pastor who keeps a large number of missionaries at work in his parish, remarked that one year he employed several theological students in this way. "How did it work?" asked a friend. "Well," he replied hesitatingly, "it was good for the students."

However much we may regret the existence of social classes in the United States, it is not wise to ignore the fact of their existence in our work. For regular pastors and preachers we want the best trained and most polished gentlemen that the schools can supply; but such men are not of the sort to get into the homes and hearts of the working-people. If they are to reach workingmen, they must be assisted by workingmen. This principle is especially important in dealing with our foreign population. It is not held that services for these people should always be conducted in their mother tongue. Most of them understand English, and English is the language of their children; but they should be approached by men who are able to look at things from their stand-point.

In Berlin the writer had the pleasure of repeated interviews with Count Pückler, an associate of Von Schlümbach, one of the most active and efficient workers in all Germany. He said that during a recent visit in the United States, he addressed, upon religious matters, large audiences of his countrymen in most of our principal cities, and that in connection with those addresses, young Germans were constantly coming to

him with the remark : "If you will organize a Christian association among us, we will support it gladly,
but we can't work with the Americans; they are too
good for us. They regard us as the greatest sinners if we
drink a glass of beer or have a fête on Sunday afternoon. They don't understand our ways, nor we theirs."

Men who have been brought up to think that beer is
as much a " staff of life " as bread itself, will not, of
course, accept total abstinence as a Christian duty at
the outset. After a prayer-meeting in the rooms of the
Berlin Young Men's Christian Association, the young
men commonly retire to a little restaurant connected
with the establishment and there discuss a glass of beer
together; and they have no notion whatever of any
incongruity between the praying and the drinking.
One reason why we have won to our churches and to
our Saviour so few of the strangers within our gates, is
because we have made so few rational efforts to win
them. When a down-town church finds its old sup-
porters moving away to the suburbs, instead of picking
up its hymn-books and hastening after them; instead
of selling its old building for a warehouse or a skating
rink and abandoning the neighborhood with its increasing multitude of dying men, except so far as the Catholics may save them, to the saloons and to the devil,
why should it not recognize the changed condition of
affairs and equip itself for doing the new kind of work
and reaping the new harvests that grow up rich and
rank on every side, by employing workers whom nature
and experience have fitted for that style of labor ?
Why should it not manfully stand its ground and expect the truth to triumph? The answer would be, the
plan is impracticable, because a church so situated can

scarcely pay its pastor, and cannot meet the expense of employing additional laborers. True enough! but is that a reason why the field should be abandoned? Does the burden of the work for such quarters belong to none but the few religious people left in them? Is the duty of all others limited to the wards in which they happen to live? Let the whole Church in city and suburb rally around the old enterprises and furnish the means by endowment or otherwise with which they may vigorously push their pressing work.

When men move from the crowded city to a pleasant suburb, or from a poorer to a more prosperous part of town, they do not leave behind them all responsibility for the moral and spiritual welfare of the region they forsake. Those who carry on their business and make their money in any city are under peculiar obligations to provide for the needs of that city; obligations from which they can never escape by choosing residences out of sight of its misery and beyond the sound of its sin. Business may often so crowd out population that old churches are wisely changed to new localities; but to abandon an old church when the neighborhood is as populous as ever, simply because the character of the people has changed, is a shame: it is false to the spirit of Christianity, for it is acting as though the Gospel were for the classes and not for the masses, and the mission of the Church were special instead of universal.

The men to be blamed, however, in such a case, are not those who cling to the old enterprise to the last and abandon it only when forced by necessity to do so. The ones most blameworthy are rather those who leave the old church in the days of its comparative prosperity and feel no more concerned for it thereafter. If we are to save our cities, we must mend our ways. We must cease withdrawing our forces from the thickest and most important points in the battle with evil. We must stop deserting every post of difficulty and danger. "He hath sounded forth a trumpet that shall never call retreat." The members of the great, rich churches that surround every city, must learn that they too have been bidden to deny themselves and take up their cross daily if they would be His disciples. Let this lesson be constantly impressed upon them until, in the light of the knowledge of it, continuous streams of consecrated wealth and consecrated workers are poured from the fine avenues and fair suburbs into the haunts of vice and godlessness.

We deem it a matter of greatest importance, especially in regions chiefly pupulated by workingmen, that there should be a large amount of Christian visitation. The mere social or charitable call is not enough. Godly men and women anointed for service by the Holy Spirit should go and preach Christ Jesus in the homes of carelessness and irreligion. When the Word is thus wisely, affectionately, and earnestly presented, it does not fail to bring forth much fruit. Many Christian visitors make the mistake of giving simply an invitation to attend church and letting the matter rest there. Now this invitation, "Come to church," is not the great burden of our message to dying men. The Bible has not much to say about it ; it does not take hold on heart and conscience, especially where the person addressed has never known a religious training. It is easily fended off. Men will say that they are too tired to attend church on Sundays, that they have no suitable clothing, that some one in the church has injured them, that they do not like the minister, that they cannot afford to pay for a seat, that family duties keep them at home. A dozen reasons are at hand to excuse them. But the great invitation, "Come to Christ," is one against which no valid excuse can ever, under any circumstances, be urged, and an excuse that even seems plausible is hard to find. This invitation goes directly to the root of the matter ; it presents at once, clearly, forcibly, and in a way that cannot be avoided, the great issue between right and wrong, between the service of God and the service of this world and its ruler. We do not, of course, mean to decry the practice of urging men to come to church, but this is after all a secondary matter and should have a secondary place. Those who rely mainly on it in their Christian work to the neglect of the direct invitation of the Gospel are like men who lay aside the keen sword and go to battle armed only with blunt sticks. Non-church-goers rarely stay away from the house of God for lack of an invitation to attend. The doors of the sanctuary, the lips of God's people, cards, dodgers, newspapers, all repeat a thousand times the invitation, "Come." But the earnest personal call to Jesus Christ is one they rarely hear. Persuade men to come to Christ first and afterward there will be no difficulty in persuading them to come to church.

American Christians may learn a valuable lesson from the work of the Sisters of Mercy and Deaconesses of England. We have the best of authority for closely connecting the cure of the diseased body with that of the sin-sick soul. "Son, thy sins are forgiven thee; take up thy bed and walk." Gifts of healing came along with those of preaching in the days of the apostles. The chief business of the church is, beyond a doubt, that of saving souls; but has she not gone too far in making that her only calling? When sickness breaks in upon a workingman's narrow home, it is a heavy affliction: helpers are few; accommodations are poor and scanty; there is little knowledge of disease and its treatment; the invalid fights for life at fearful disadvantage. Where one dies for want of medicine, ten perish for lack of care and nursing.

If the church had a corps of saintly women trained to nursing, so that she could send one of them like a ministering angel into every afflicted household, by what cords of love she might bind its members to herself! When men are in trouble their hearts are soft; the love you show them then, and the help you offer, are not soon forgotten. Cold victuals and old clothes may be acceptable when people are hard pressed and the wolf is at the door; but how rarely have such presents brought the receiver by a single step nearer to the Saviour. Even the giving of money is a dangerous experiment: while affording to the needy temporary relief, it is apt to do so at the heavy cost of self-respect, and to push them on toward pauperism. But when one offers himself or some loved member of his family to the service of the poor, there is a gift which can neither degrade nor pauperize, but can only ennoble and bless those that give and those that take.

Speaking of sisterhoods, Bishop Ireland, of Minnesota, says: "We claim peculiar advantages from the system of Catholic charities. It secures in the service of charity what is most valuable and most difficult to be obtained,—the sweetness and tenderness of love. It is not bread or medicine that is most prized by the indigent and the sick : it is the smile and the soft caress, the kind, hopeful word. The heart rather than the mouth must be fed : the soul rather than the body must be warmed. All this is done without effort, and is done with exquisite delicacy, when the heart of the laborer is in his work. The Catholic brother and sister are inspired by love. They could not endure the religious life unless the heart were all on fire with love: love streams from the heart and ignites all other hearts coming within the circle of its influence."

Shall the advantages of such a system be monopolized by those who have so little else to offer? Where can the churches find a better way of winning to themselves and their Lord, the hearts of His poor? Were it needful, they would do well to fill their windows with plain glass and let their floors go bare, rather than pass heedlessly by such open doors of opportunity.

II. A few words as to the nature and frequency of religious services which should be provided for the masses. A religion for working-people must be vital. It must present in their simplest, most direct form the great verities of our faith. The less they realize it, the more true it is that they hunger for the bread of life. That service is, therefore, best adapted to their needs which provides the fullest supply, not of literature, philosophy, theology art or music, but plain Gospel truth. Now the truth never comes to men so powerfully as from the lips of a fellow-man in whom it lives and who lives in it : no set form of words can so lift up the soul of the congregation into fellowship with God, as the spontaneous prayer of one whose petitions spring from the suggestion of God's indwelling Spirit. Taking both at their best, the non-liturgical churches, there-

fore, seem to us better adapted to the needs of the
common people than those which lean on the staff of a
ritual; and it is our impression, although this would
hardly be acknowledged by a "churchman," that the
religious history and life of England verifies this position. Notwithstanding the great advantages that the
Established Church has had in dealing with the common people because of its endowments and prestige,
the fact that it need not appeal to its adherents for
financial support, and that it has much more money to
spend for charity,—it will hardly be denied that the
nonconformists of various sects have been more successful in engaging the hearts of the humbler classes
than the Establishment.

On the other hand, a cripple can walk better with a
staff than without it. If there be no spiritual life in
the church or its minister, the service is far more acceptable when it takes the form of a majestic ritual
which the coldest of readers cannot altogether rob of
truth and strength, than when it depends for inspiration and helpfulness upon the utterances of one whose
prayers have no uplifting power. Heat will not come
out of one who is cold, nor can a dead man give life to
others. The church without the liturgy, if it be dead,
is the deadest of all dead churches. The first great
requisite for success with the people, the lack of which
cannot be supplied by any kind of attraction or contrivance, is, therefore, *life.*

There can be no doubt, however, that the methods of
service which are wisest, vary with the varying conditions of those for whom they are designed. What
suited the keen logicians of the New England farms a
century ago would hardly be the thing for a popular

13

audience in a modern factory town.   We may well ask
ourselves whether the elements of instruction and persuasion have not, even now, places of too great relative
prominence in the Sabbath service of most churches in
comparison with that which is given to worship. There
is something deeply impressive in the fondness of the
Englishman for his church. He is, if we are not mistaken, a much more faithful and punctual attendant at
the house of God than the American. He does not go
for the sake of fashion and vanity, for he dresses plainly, nor for the sake of hearing the sermon, for he makes
it a matter of secondary importance ; but for the
service. Into this he enters with all his heart. People
love a service in which they feel that they have a personal part. Is not the minister's part too great with
us, and that of the people too small? Have we not
made a mistake, for instance, in giving up the response
to prayer and hymn, the audible "amen," whereby each
worshipper endorses and adopts for himself the peti-
tion of the leader?

Singing is the one way in which a whole congregation may most freely and naturally unite in the worship
of God. It exalts the feelings, warms the affections,
and flings open to the truth the chambers of the soul.
In thousands of cases a song has been the first thing
to touch a man's heart. It is said that Wesleyanism,
the religion of common people, "sang its way around
the world." In order to reach the masses, there must
be plenty of good music in which all can engage.
Many London churches do not think five congregational hymns too many for an ordinary morning service.
What could be more quenching to the spirit of praise
than the custom of sitting in one's seat and listening to

the artistic trills and quavers of mercenary musicians, instead of standing up to "praise the living God with heart and soul and voice"?

Our English brethren do well in having more frequent religious services than we. In order that people may feel deeply, think strongly, and act rightly in matters of religion, its great truths should be kept constantly before them. As the protracted meeting nourishes the revival spirit, so continuous meetings give to religion a perennial life. Frequent services are of special importance among humble people. John Wesley used to say that the idea of holding meetings less often than every day originated with the devil. A large part of the success with which the Salvation Army retains its influence over those that join it, is due to the frequency of its services. The evenings of workingmen are largely on their hands; their homes are not attractive; they have little taste for reading; after the monotonous toil and confinement of the day they naturally spend the evening abroad. The cheap places of public amusement whose open doors invite them, are likely to be most unwholesome. When a church stands in the midst of such a populace, it ought never to be closed of an evening. Not that the people should be urged to attend church every day in the week, but that there should always be some sort of a bright, short, interesting service that they can attend if they choose. Here is one of the points in which we see the pressing need of increasing the working force of the city churches.

The character of such daily services could wisely be diversified so as to suit the various elements in the congregation. There are some who enjoy simple melodies

like those introduced by Mr. Sankey, brief prayers,
stirring testimonies, and short, pointed appeals. Another element is better helped by services in which
there is more of refinement and less of enthusiasm. No
one style will suit all sorts and conditions of men
equally well. Why, then, should the church conduct
every meeting on the same plan? Let some of them
take the popular complexion and use the Gospel songs.
Let others be of more conservative type, and make use
of the classical hymns of the church. A mid-week
service, with preaching or lecture, would doubtless be
as useful here as it has proven in England. The young
people with their special prayer-meeting, or their "Society of Christian Endeavor," could make good use of
one evening in the week, and a Gospel temperance
meeting may well be planted in the midst of the drunkenness of every Saturday night.

But not only should religious meetings be more frequent than has usually been the case, they should also,
for the best effect, be somewhat scattered throughout
the community which it is desired to reach. It is an
opinion which we believe to be daily growing upon the
convictions of those most interested in such matters,
that a given amount of religious energy is better and
more economically expended in many small meetings
than in few large ones.* While concentration is the
watchword of modern life in other things, that of religion seems to be dispersion. The more thoroughly
the leaven is mixed with the meal, the sooner the whole

---

* See Report of Special Committee on City Evangelization, made
to the American Home Missionary Society at their annual meeting at
Saratoga, June 8, 1887, printed in full in the *Christian Union*,
June 16.

will be leavened; the more widely scattered the seed, the more abundant the harvest; many little nets catch more than few great ones. Those who could never be persuaded to attend church will readily consent to go into the little meeting in the neighbor's parlor. But such little meetings are the very places where the personal claims of Jesus Christ may be most closely, powerfully, and effectively presented. They afford the church an unsurpassed opportunity for setting its most consecrated members at work. Heart comes closer to heart in the little room. Hand grasps hand; kind and helpful words are easily spoken. It is a good place for the young convert's first confession of Christ. There is little opportunity for unhealthful excitement. The minimum of effort brings the maximum of result. The days of monster evangelistic meetings we believe to be numbered; the simpler, quieter, and more continuous methods have proven more effective. The new evangelism does not build gigantic tabernacles to be crowded for a month and then forsaken, but it plants permanent churches in needy districts, which stretch out their hands on all sides through multitudes of little meetings held in halls, shops, school-buildings, homes, and tenement-houses, to gather to themselves multitudes of such as shall be saved.

It is a question worth considering whether we could not make more frequent and effective use than we do of the sacrament of the Lord's Supper. Although this sacred ordinance is by no means a mass, is not a sacrifice, and has in itself no purifying power for the sake of which we sinners have frequent need of it,—it is a visible memorial of the great sacrifice whereby we live. Seeing that it speaks of the one central event of

history and religion with a power and eloquence which
no human lips can rival, is there any reason why its
symbolic voice should not be heard oftener and more
openly?

III. The work of the English churches suggests, as a
third topic for remark, the efficiency of the parish
system.

There are two distinct systems on which the religious
life of a town may proceed : either the town may be
divided into a number of distinct districts or parishes,
a church planted in each and that church made solely
responsible for the religious instruction of every household in its own parish—or, the churches may be located
without special reference to the needs of their immediate neighborhood, in such spots as appear desirable,
and may make it their aim to attract to themselves as
many as possible from all parts of the town, each church
counting as parishioners those and those only who
accept its invitations and attend its services.   The
former is the system practiced, in theory at least, by
the Established Church of England.   The latter is that
which generally prevails among the Nonconformists
and in the United States.   The immense advantages of
the parish system in conducting the religious work of
large towns are obvious.   This system places a distinct
and definite work before every church and thus gives
to all religious effort the vast advantage of having a
specific rather than a general aim.   It has been well
said that "every general arrangement with reference
to a whole is impotent in comparison with a special
arrangement adapted to the needs of a special part."
It makes somebody directly responsible for every family in the city, and the whole field may thus be thor-

oughly overlooked by the churches ; the moral and religious condition of every household in it known; the exact number of irreligious persons discovered, and prayer and effort put forth for the conversion of each. The inroads of vice may be watched; temptation nipped in the bud; evil prevented from massing itself and thus increasing its power—and the whole body of society may be thoroughly permeated with the salt of Christian influence. Above all, the parish system of church work surpasses the other because it leaves little or no room for those rivalries and jealousies between competing churches which are the shame of Protestantism. Its value has been powerfully set forth by Dr. Chalmers and was strikingly illustrated by him both in Glasgow and Edinburgh. Scarcely a man since the days of the Apostles could have spoken with greater weight of authority upon such a theme than he.

The other system, the one that prevails almost exclusively in our own cities, builds up, indeed, large and flourishing churches which worship in beautiful buildings, listen to eloquent sermons, and make generous contributions to missions ; but the trouble with them is, that their work is superficial and partial; they deal with only a small, selected portion of the population and leave the rest uncared for. Such churches minister to none except those who choose to attend them, but they who stand in greatest need of their ministrations are the last to make such a choice.

"In proportion to our want of food is our desire for food; but it is not so with our want of knowledge or virtue or religion. The more destitute we are of these last, the more dead we are to any inclination for them. In moving through the lanes and recesses of a long-neglected population, it would be found of the fearful multitude that not only is their acquaintance with the Gospel extinguished, but their desire to obtain an acquaintance with it is also extinguished." *

Such people will never come to church of their own accord, and consequently can never be reached by a church that counts as belonging to its parish and under its charge, those families and those only whose members are attracted to its services. There are tens of thousands in every great city in the land whom no possible degree of attractiveness could persuade to attend church. Make your seats as free, your invitations as cordial, your house as beautiful, your music as fine, and your preaching as eloquent as you please—they will not think of coming. Could a saloon-keeper, by refurnishing his place and improving the quality of his liquors, persuade the Christian public to become his patrons?

It is true that the more you increase your attractions the larger your audiences will become and the more flourishing your church will appear, but none of this increase will come from the class which needs the Gospel most. How close is the application to our cities, of words which Chalmers uttered more than half a century ago :

"There is room enough for apparent Christianity and real corruption to be gaining ground together, each in their respective territories; and the delusion is that while many are rejoicing in the symptoms of our country's reformation, the country itself may

---

* *The Christian and Civic Economy of Large Towns.* Thomas Chalmers, Glasgow, p. 62.

be ripening for some awful crisis by which to mark in characters of vengeance the consummation of its guilt." *

It is high time to cease depending upon the attractiveness of songs and sermons in cushioned and carpeted sanctuaries: if we are to save the lost we must go out and seek them, for they will not come back of themselves. Many have reached this conclusion and have attempted going out into the highways and compelling men to come in, but they have met an almost insuperable difficulty at the outset. Being resolved to go, the first question is, where? The city has tens and hundreds of thousands of non church-goers living everywhere. The individual church is but a little company of a few hundred and contains no more than a score or two of active and willing workers who are widely scattered. These workers usually proceed without much method in their attempt to bring non-church-goers to the sanctuary; their efforts are consequently scattered and largely wasted. The very vastness of the work that presses in upon every side paralyzes many and many a city church into a state of languor and inactivity. The sense of their utter inability to lift the whole awful burden of the great towns' sin and sorrow is so overpowering, that they grow discouraged, attempt none of it, and are fain to be contented with waging the inglorious warfare of self-preservation.

Now this difficulty could surely be overcome if each church would make its work strictly local. Instead of vainly striving to shoulder the whole community at

---

* Ibid, p. 66.

once, or standing idle and despondent at its inability to do so, let every church take charge of a fixed and definite portion of the town, of a size proportionate to its strength, and then let it, in direct and systematic fashion, concentrate its efforts upon that corner of the vineyard. " Thus a church of moderate ability, without members of special talent or great wealth, and without peculiarly favorable circumstances, can, as has been proved repeatedly by experience, sensibly elevate the moral, intellectual, and physical condition of any community to which it puts its hand "

It may seem strange that a method of work so obviously wise and effective should so rarely be put into practice by our American churches; but the reason for this is, alas! equally obvious. The forces of the kingdom of heaven are scattered and divided between a score and more of rival sects, no one of which will allow to another exclusive right to any portion of territory, no matter how little it may be doing there itself. One cannot start a mission Sunday-school in a destitute neighborhood without being suspected of trying to seize the ground, not for Christ's sake, but for some denomination. The few Christian people living in such a community who would naturally be expected to support the new movement, cannot do so, because they belong to churches of half a dozen different orders. They will not heartily enter into any enterprise except one that is called by their own name. If you attempt to call upon the families of some neglected and godless quarter of the town, and to press upon its ignorant and reckless people the claims of God and the invitations of His church, you must be very careful to ascertain, before visiting a household, that none of its children attend any Sunday-school except your own; for, if so, alas! you are a proselyter.

In their influence upon the common people, especially those of foreign birth, the schisms of our churches are productive of incalculable mischief. In contrast with our division, the Roman Catholic Church points triumphantly to her unity. Her point is well taken by them, for they do not see and cannot realize that her unity is that of death, all agreeing because one thinks for all; while underneath our seeming diversity there thrills and throbs the mightier unity of life. Amid the various calls and invitations of the different churches they do not detect one spirit and a single aim. The voice of the bride is so broken, confused, and bewildering, that they fail to hear her, and over her sectaries and schisms, myriads go stumbling headlong into hell.

If the authority of every Christian in the city—nay, of the church universal—could be concentrated for a man into the single voice of his own parish church, how mightily would her summons appeal to his heart! Has not the time fully come, brethren, when every man who loves the kingdom of God should set his face like a flint against the present disastrous system—a system based upon the untenable and long since abandoned position that discipleship and fellowship depend upon agreement in doctrinal opinion rather than upon common participation in the life of Christ? Who is so foolish in our day as to suppose that living, thinking men can all be made to think alike? As to the great facts of our faith, we are already one. As to minor points of polity and doctrine, there is neither hope nor need that we should agree. Why not agree to disagree? The times demand no new sect which shall attempt to swallow up all others; no national church or interference of civil authority in ecclesiastical matters, but a federation of all churches that believe Jesus Christ is the Son of God, of all that love His name and daily pray "Thy kingdom come." It is not enough that the denominations have friendly feelings toward one another, and exchange compliments in occasional union meetings; the exigencies of these days call aloud for nothing less than a unity of plan on the part of the entire working force of Christ's Church. Let us cease our rivalry and wrangling, put away our absurd pretensions to a monopoly of wisdom and truth, divide the territory among us, and put our shoulder to the work; for the day is far spent, the night is at hand, and the world, still cursed by sin and darkened by death, groaneth and travaileth, weary with long waiting for the day of her redemption.

IV. Our final suggestion shall be the importance of cultivating in the churches a spirit of sympathy with workingmen which is broader, truer, and more profoundly Christian than that now prevalent. Christianity, in its onward march, has obliterated invidious distinctions between Jew and Greek, male and female, bond and free; still more, would one expect to find in the body of the church, at least, an equal footing for rich and poor. Yet such is not the case.

When one remembers to what condition of life the great Head of the Church chose to be born, how that a stable was the scene of His nativity, His kindred and friends were but peasants, and He himself a common carpenter, it appears incredible that people of lowly birth should ever have been disdained by His followers; yet many professing Christians do thoroughly ignore the bonds of human brotherhood which unite them with the working-people; they give themselves no concern for their physical, intellectual, or spiritual welfare; they take all pains to exclude themselves from their society, both at home and in the house of God; they avoid all contact with them, except that which must exist between master and servant, and they behave as though they esteemed them an inferior sort of creature scarcely to be mentioned in the same breath with themselves and those of their rank. Of such persons, we scarcely need observe that they have not the spirit of Christ, for Christian love is universal; it overleaps every fence of class distinction, and receives all sorts and conditions of men into its broad embrace. But a very large proportion of the efforts of those who do spend their time and money for the poorer classes, are painfully barren of permanent and substantial benefit, because the spirit from which such efforts spring, and with which they are thoroughly permeated, is something less and lower than the true Christian spirit.

What with their missions, ragged-schools, refuges, tract distributers, hospitals, and charitable institutions of all sorts, the number of enterprises supported by Christian philanthropy in London is well-nigh countless; yet it cannot be said that the Christian religion—not, at any rate, that the Christian Church—has a very strong hold upon the working-people in that city; they are poorly represented in the churches, compared with the middle and upper classes.

The writer had a long talk on the subject with Mr. J. J. Dent, General Secretary for England of the Workingmen's Club and Institute Union. He is a keen, clearly-speaking, thoughtful man, is thoroughly conversant with the ways and opinions of the working-classes, and as good an authority on such matters as could be found. He said that among Protestants in London and in all English towns, the work-ing-people are largely alienated from the churches, especially from the Established Church, but also from those of the Nonconformists. He gave it as his opinion that the chief reason for such alienation was no lack of attention paid by the churches to the workingman, no lack of missions and charities, but it was rather owing to the aristocratic spirit in which the men conceive themselves to be approached by the churches.

"The workingmen," said he, "do not want to be treated as protégés or paupers; they cannot bear to be patronized; all they ask of religious people is to be treated on the basis of humanity and justice."

The spirit of the patron is not that of the brother; it does not spring from love, but from some mixed motive: partly sense of duty, partly mean arrogance and base conceit. It implies an inherent superiority on the part of one man over another, an implication false to a cardinal doctrine of Christianity—the glorious truth that the human soul is in and of itself precious, and, like the diamond, takes its value not from setting, cut, or polish, but from intrinsic worth. Who can blame an honest, self-respecting man if he fails to appreciate favors that are bound up with implied insults, if he receives religion coldly when she presents herself in the hateful garb of patronage?

It is hard to see how one can present the truths of the Gospel in the patronizing spirit without incurring the gravest suspicions of insincerity. Can you offer to share with a man on equal terms that which you really believe to be your best possession and your highest dignity, and at the same time look down upon him as an inferior? Whoever hopes to lead any man to Christ must approach him in the affectionate and respectful spirit of a brother. When we offer him our greatest and best things, let us not withhold small ones. If he be permitted to share with us the paternal love of God, the sacrifice of Christ, and the power of the Holy Ghost—shall we count our cushions, carpets, organs, and comfortable pews too good for him? Shall we banish him to cheerless chapels with bare floor and hard seats? If we are sincere in inviting him to be a brother in Christ, we must treat him and his children as members of the family when he accepts the invitation.

Our interest in the working-classes must be more comprehensive. A true Christian love does not confine itself to one's spiritual and eternal interests, but extends to the whole man. Too often has the Church behaved toward the masses as though there were nothing about them worth considering except their immortal souls. Efforts are put forth for their conversion, tracts distributed, special meetings held, they are urged to come to Christ and to join His church, but interest in them ends here.

"You promise us plenty of heaven hereafter, but you rob us of all but a pittance here," cries the socialist bitterly. "Keep your heaven to yourself and give us a fair share of the good things of this life."

Has he not some slender thread of truth on which to hang this scathing charge? It is quite impossible to make one believe that you love his soul when you seem indifferent to his body; that you are anxious to have him secure a heavenly home when you give yourself no concern regarding his earthly dwelling. Men know that a real love confines itself to no part or portion of the one beloved, but includes his whole life and being. Now the workingman, beholding this apparently one-sided sort of interest in him, casts about for an explanation, and it is not hard to find a plausible one. There are many rival churches in a community, every one of which is ambitious to become the largest and most prosperous. All are eager to add as many as possible to their roll of membership. They would like to count him as a convert. Is this why they are so anxious for the salvation of his soul?

The English are wiser than we, in that they have established more points of contact between the church and the common people. If we are brothers in religion, we are brothers in all things. Why should not the brotherhood of the church assist the poor woman in buying tea or coal, the unemployed laborer in finding a situation, or provide the easily-tempted lad with some healthful recreation for his evenings? Why should it not encourage thrift by starting penny banks and friendly societies where they are needed? Why not evening-schools, cheap concerts, exhibitions of art and popular lectures, as well as prayer-meetings and Gospel services?

Those who work most wisely among the poor are sparing with their alms and lavish with their friendship. To help a man by the gift of money, food, or clothing, is almost certain to degrade him; to help him by the gift of time, thought, and brotherly love, uplifts him. The people should always be taught and expected to bear a share in the expense of any enterprise undertaken for their benefit. Whatever is free is lightly valued.

The working-classes are doubtless better situated in the United States than in any other country on earth, and they are perhaps as prosperous, on the whole, to-day, as they have been in former years; yet how widely removed is their condition from what one would choose for himself or a loved member of his family! Those who practice the golden rule are not satisfied with their situation :—the degrading machine toil, not too hard, perhaps, but tediously dull ; the close, disagreeable homes; the sharp, continuous struggle with poverty; the dreadful anxiety, like that of a man who walks in the dark on a precipice's edge, caused by the knowledge that some business depression, strike, or accident may any day rob him of work, and bring him to destitution ; the hopelessness of life that begins to come upon us, reaching the poorest first : as the nation grows older, its lines harden into fixedness, and the doors of opportunity that once made every young man's path so full of hope, close one by one, leaving it more and more difficult for him to rise out of the station to which he was born; above all, the inevitable blindness and deafness to those things that give us so much of our best enjoyment: art, music, and letters,—the world of beauty and the world of thought. When men so situated, in dim, half instinctive consciousness of a royal birthright which hard necessity has forced them to barter for the mess of pottage, try to rise and regain their priceless inheritance, shall the Church turn toward them the cold shoulder? God forbid ! Though their methods be not those of wisdom ; though they blindly follow worthless leaders, and violently blame the guiltless for their misfortunes, let us never scorn them nor their cause, but hear them respectfully and cordially, giving our best wisdom to the solution of their difficulties. As soon as these people know that we love them, so soon shall we begin to win them.

No words can tell, brethren, no words can commence to tell how tremendous is the importance of giving to our working-people the knowledge of God through Jesus Christ. As water cannot be boiled by applying heat at the top, so society cannot be saved by a religion of the upper classes. The present religious condition of the cities is of necessity a temporary one : the fire must burn down to the bottom or the fire must go out. Christianity, from the nature of it, cannot remain the religion of a class : it must be the religion of the whole people or that of none. There have been Christian nations before now from whom the light of the knowledge of God has faded quite away

The men that rule, in our country at least, usually spring from the ranks of the lowly. They are not delicately brought up nor clothed in soft raiment. They are men who inherit iron constitutions from fathers used to toil and sweat ; men whom early hardships have taught patience and endurance ; who amid the difficulties of poverty have grown strong with struggling. The humble homes which have hitherto sent out such men have oftenest been homes of piety, familiar with God's word and the voice of prayer. But these humble homes, both in the country and in town, have now for many years been fast passing into the hands of strangers. What if our future leaders are being reared in Roman Catholic households, and cradled by the firesides of unbelief? Woe to the nation whose cottages have no Bibles!

The poor and the stranger must be taught to know the God of our fathers : it is our only hope. This only hope is a large hope. The Gospel was made for the poor—they need it, they hunger for it, they will receive it when it is faithfully preached. The Church is bidden to go with her messages of life. There is a promise that the Word will not be fruitless. Wherever Christ goes, Christ wins. He has done greater things than these. The chief danger lies in the unbelief of His people; in the shameful assumption that because the poor are foreigners and Catholics they cannot be brought to Jesus. Those who have tried it know better. " All things are possible with God."

Have you no vision, dear reader, of a man who stands amid the bustling multitudes of some great town, rough-coated and begrimed by the touch of toil, but with a pleading face and a beckoning hand? And does there never reach your ears above all the noises of the city's uproar, a cry, " Come and help us ! " The cry of humanity is the call of God. " He that hath an ear to hear, let him hear."

INDEX.